International Research on Poverty Reduction

Volume 1

Series Editors

Xiaolin Wang
International Poverty Reduction Center in China
Beijing, China

Qianqian Liu
International Poverty Reduction Center in China
Beijing, China

For further volumes:
http://www.springer.com/series/11685

International Research on Poverty Reduction

Poverty remains a crucial development issue for the world, and China has become an important player in the global endeavor in poverty reduction and development. China has made a substantial contribution to the achievement of the Millennium Development Goals (MDGs) by reducing half of its poverty population. This book series discuss themes such as poverty reduction practices and experience; knowledge mobilization; poverty reduction strategy analysis; comparative research of different poverty reduction models etc. By analyzing China's poverty reduction approaches and experiences, and comparing them with those of other countries, this book series wishes to provide policy makers, researchers and practitioners in poverty reduction with theoretical and technical support, and to provide a new channel for sharing experiences as well as facilitating collaboration and communication in poverty reduction development fields between China and the rest of the world.

Xiaolin Wang • Limin Wang • Yan Wang

The Quality of Growth and Poverty Reduction in China

SSAP

Springer

Xiaolin Wang
International Poverty Reduction
Center in China
Beijing 100028, China

Limin Wang
The World Bank
Washington, DC 20433, USA

Yan Wang
George Washington University
Washington, DC 20052, USA

ISSN 2195-9781 ISSN 2195-979X (electronic)
ISBN 978-3-642-36345-0 ISBN 978-3-642-36346-7 (eBook)
DOI 10.1007/978-3-642-36346-7
Springer Heidelberg New York Dordrecht London

Library of Congress Control Number: 2014937805

Printed on acid-free paper

Springer is part of Springer Science+Business Media (www.springer.com)

Sponsored by the Chinese Fund for the Humanities and Social Sciences

Acknowledgments

This policy report draws on the academic background paper prepared by a team under the overall guidance of Dr. Xiaolin Wang, Director of Research Division of the International Poverty Reduction Center in China (IPRCC) for the 5th China-ASEAN Forum on Poverty Reduction and Social Development. The core team, led by Xiaolin Wang, includes Dr. Deliang Zhang, Liping Xu, and Min Yu.

Many others within IPRCC provided helpful comments. Valuable advice was received from internal peer reviewers Dr. Chengwei Huang (Deputy Director General), Xiaojun He (Deputy Director General), Dr. Enjiang Cheng (Senior Technical Specialist), Dr. Linyi Li (Project Officer), Ms. Xiaoying Zhang (Project Officer), Liping Xu (Project Officer) and Min Yu (Postdoctoral).

We are grateful to Liping Xu for excellent research assistance, Sabrina Snell (IPRCC Intern) for editing, and Dr. Salehuddin Ahmed (Chief Technical Advisor, IPRCC), Dr. Qianqian Liu (Project Officer, IPRCC), Jiming Zhu (IPRCC Intern), and Liyu Qiu (IPRCC Intern) for polishing and proofreading.

Special thanks to all the publishing editors, production editors and copy editors from Springer and Ms. Li Zhou, Shasha Cai, Wei Yun and all other related editors from Social Science Academic Press (China).

Finally, the team gratefully acknowledges the support from Dr. Vinod Thomas, Director General of Evaluation, Asian Development Bank.

The findings, interpretations, and conclusions expressed in this book are those of the authors and do not necessarily represent the views of the International Poverty Reduction Center in China.

Main Messages

Over the past few decades, many developing countries have been trying to make the transformation from agrarian and resource-based economies to industrialized and technology-driven economies through rapid, inclusive, and sustainable growth. Some of them have failed, but a few countries have succeeded. Among the developing countries from 1960 to 2010 that were studied by the Growth Commission, only 13 economies were able to sustain an average growth rate of 7 % for a period of over a decade (Growth Commission Report 2009). China was the only country that has made three historical transformations: from a centralized planning system to a market-oriented economy, from a closed economy to an open and export-oriented one, and from an agrarian economy to a manufacturing center of the world. In the course of these transformations, more than 660 million people have been lifted above the World Bank poverty line of $1.25 per person per day, and China has integrated with the global economies through the exchange of goods and services, financial resources, human capital, and technology. In short, China has risen above poverty and transformed beyond its boundaries during the past three decades' sustained rapid growth.

However, experience of the successful emerging developing countries, in particular, China, reaffirms that it is the quality of growth, with its emphasis on growth rate, poverty reduction, equity, and environmental and resource sustainability that promote development and improve well-being. The global experiences show that a narrow focus on the pace of economic growth can hinder economic development or even reverse social progress. More alarmingly, the blind pursuit of rapid growth can eventually bring a country to the brink of environmental catastrophe, limiting any prospect of future growth and harming the welfare of its population.

Economic growth in itself is not sufficient to achieve social progress, and the role of government in providing basic public goods, addressing inequality and bad externalities such as pollution is critical. The goal of development lies in expanding capability through improvement in health and education and promoting equity and equality of opportunities—ultimately providing freedoms and rights to people to participate in economic and social life. The rapid growth of the past three decades was instrumental in lifting over 660 million people out of income poverty in China. But growth in itself does not guarantee achieving desirable development outcomes.

However, the progressive social policies and government-led investment in social services and rural development before the 1980s underpinned China's success in achieving impressive human development outcomes in health, education, and gender equality with very low level of per capita income. As China experienced an unprecedented growth, with per capita income rising by over 16 times, the role of government in social services provision diminished and improvement in health outcomes stalled. Consequently, social disparities in health and education began to widen while gender inequality likewise deteriorated. Despite the intimate connection between income disparities and growth during a country's transformation into an industrialized economy, inequality in China has risen to an alarming level and poses a serious threat to social and political stability.

As a result of its economic reforms, open-door polices, and integration into the global economy, China has seen growth unmatched by any other country in history. In the first two decades of China's reform, economic growth was largely driven by productivity growth, resulting from more efficient resource allocation as the centrally planned system was replaced by a more market-oriented economy. The productivity growth also came from production and technology upgrading through the restructuring of SOEs and technology transfers brought about by FDI and industry policies such as those creating special economic zones. The integration into the global economy through trade, FDI, and exchange of people provided a catalyst to spur growth by allowing China to explore its comparative advantages in low-cost labors and economies of scale. Government-led development, both in hard infrastructure (such as roads, telecommunication networks, and access electricity) and soft infrastructure (such as knowledge, information, management skills, and the development of a set of legal and regulatory institutional framework), provided a business-friendly climate that was crucial to sustaining growth.

How can China raise "the efficiency and the quality" of its growth through structural transformation? That is a fundamental question confronted by all in the next decade. To sustain growth and ensure the benefits of growth are shared more equally, China must advance its structural transformation. China's first two decades of growth between 1978–2000 are marked by the transformation from an agriculture-based economy to one dominated by industry and services sectors and a process of rapid urbanization. The majority of Chinese people benefited from this inclusive pattern of growth through expanded employment opportunities. However, the pattern of growth in the past decade between 2000–2012 has been accompanied by major structural imbalances, namely, an excessive capital accumulation and weak domestic consumption, an over-dominating industrial sector and underdeveloped services sector, and a skewed national income distribution (with enterprises and the government taking a disproportionate share of national income while households' portion became progressively smaller). Despite being the second largest economy in the world, China lagged behind in knowledge-intensive and high-technology industries and services. In the twenty-first century, an educated labor force combined with advancement in science and technology and innovation, rather than just abundant energy and resources, underpins sustained growth and prosperity. China must advance its transformation to sustain growth and remain competitive—moving from low value-added and energy-intensive manufacturing to high value-added industries and services. This requires economic policies focusing on the promotion of science and technology and innovation and on the accumulation of human capital.

China plays a critical role in addressing the two greatest global issues of our time: poverty reduction and climate change. Despite China's success in achieving a rapid growth and massive reduction of extreme poverty, it is still home to about a seventh of the world's poor. Scaling up targeted antipoverty development programs and government social spending in improving health and education, together with promoting an inclusive pattern of growth by expanding employment opportunities to the poor segments of the population, can further reduce poverty in China, and thus globally. In combating global warming, China plays a pivotal role, not only because it surpassed the United States to become the world's largest emitter of greenhouse gas, but also because it has been the world's leading renewable energy producer and investor in renewable energy technologies. The development targets set in China's 12th Five-Year Plan emphasizing energy efficiency, renewable energy sources, and environmental protection, if achieved, can bring enormous economic and environmental benefits both to Chinese population and the rest of the world.

Environmental and resource sustainability must be placed at the centre of economic growth discourse and policymaking. International evidence made it clear that a global economy based on current patterns of consumption and production is simply not sustainable. Policymakers have been advised repeatedly that economic growth, poverty reduction, equity, and environmental and resource sustainability must be integrated into the development of national strategies. In reality, however, as illustrated in China's three decades of growth experience, pursuing fast growth at great costs has always been the single most important national policy that overrides other development objectives and social concerns, reflecting the intrinsically political nature of policymaking. The severe environment and resource degradation resulting from the pursuit of fast growth at great costs will bring negative consequences to the Chinese population and its future generations. While some environment and resource degradation might be reversible, the potentially enormous cost of cleaning up and depletion of natural resources, in particular, water, will impede future growth. Future generations in China have already been deprived of the opportunities to live in a safe and clean environment and an ecosystem with biodiversity.

Looking forward, this book provides us with cause for optimism about China's development over the coming decades. The new generation of Chinese leaders and the government have set out an ambitious and comprehensive agenda in structural reforms in the "Decision by the Third Plenum Session of the Chinese Communist Party" held in 2013. In addition to rebalancing the economy, mitigating social inequality, protecting the environment, and addressing climate change, addressing rural-urban divide and improving the quality of growth are placed high in the policy agenda. Its commitment to achieving these goals is demonstrated through the implementation of a wide range of social policies and programs in both rural and urban areas and massive investment in clean technology and production upgrading. Meanwhile, China has become the world's leading renewable energy producer and investor. It is the hope of both the Chinese people and the rest of world to see a rising China that embarks on a development path that is equitable, sustainable, and low carbon, setting an example of successful social and economic transformation for other countries.

Contents

Chapter 1
Introduction and Overview

Sustained and rapid income growth is a modern phenomenon that appeared only after the Industrial Revolution in the eighteenth century. Before that time, for a long period, almost all countries in the world had agrarian economies, and the income gaps among countries were small. The Industrial Revolution led to accelerated growth in the Western European economies, the United States, and other Western offshoots, but most other countries failed to do so (Maddison 2010). As a consequence, there has been great divergence in income levels between developed and developing countries. By the end of the twentieth century, the gap had significantly widened, with per capita income of industrialized countries at more than 50 times that of low-income countries (Maddison 2010). Among the set of developing countries, only a handful were successful in transforming their agrarian economies into an industrialized one. Among them were Japan and the East Asian tigers.

The growth poles in the past were all high-income countries such as Germany, Japan, the United Kingdom, and the United States. In the 1980s and 1990s, among the top five contributors to global growth, all but China were industrialized countries. By 2009, all except the United States were emerging economies. The sheer size of the large emerging economies combined with their dynamic and sustained growth has elevated Brazil, Russia, India, and China (the BRIC) to become the largest contributors to global economic growth, generating over 45 % of global GDP growth. The era of a multipolar world seems to have been firmly established (Chandra et al. 2013, p. 54). China, in particular, after 33 years of rapid economic growth and structural transformation, has grown to become a manufacturing powerhouse, the largest exporter, and the second largest economy in the world.

The growth experiences from a large number of countries over the past several decades, in particular China, highlight that both the pace and pattern of growth are critical for achieving desirable development outcomes. While fast economic growth is essential to lift poor people out of poverty,[1] some growth patterns are more effective

---

[1] The 2010 OECD study also shows that extreme poverty persists in many parts of the world, despite the fact that world gross domestic product (GDP) has increased by roughly 60 % since 1992.

X. Wang et al., *The Quality of Growth and Poverty Reduction in China*,
International Research on Poverty Reduction, DOI 10.1007/978-3-642-36346-7_1,

than others in reducing poverty, improving well-being, and promoting equity.[2] And some growth patterns can generate fast economic growth while safeguarding environment, conserving natural resources and ecosystem, and emitting less carbon. It is the quality of growth that ultimately advances development and improves welfare.

1.1 The Quality Growth Framework

The quality growth framework developed by Thomas et al. (2000, 2008)[3] emphasizes three key aspects of growth, namely, poverty reduction, equality, and environmental sustainability.

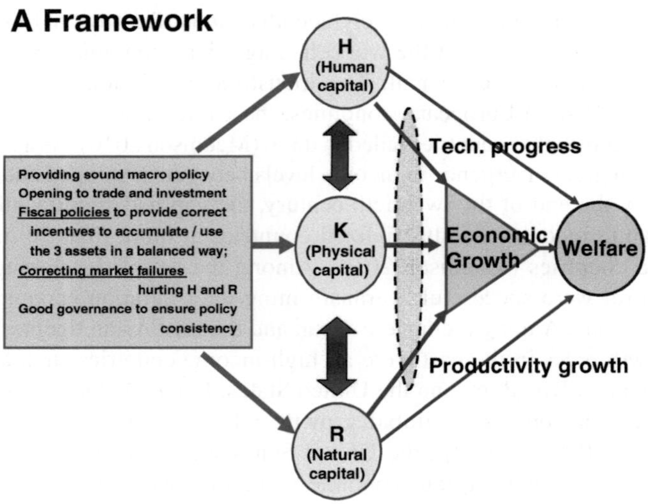

Source: Thomas et al. (2000)

Broadly speaking, countries are endowed with at least three types of assets that matter for growth and welfare: human and social capital, natural and environmental capital, and physical and financial capital. Technological progress and the institutional environment that affect the use of these assets also affect growth and welfare.

Based on cross-country comparisons, a number of papers in the literature have found that measures of absolute poverty tend to fall with economic growth (Montalvo and Ravallion 2010).

[2] See, for example, Ravallion and Chen (2004), Christiaensen et al. (2006), Loayza and Raddatz (2006), World Bank (2005), and the Annual Review of Development Effectiveness (IEG 2007a) and the Development Results in Middle-Income Countries Report (IEG 2007b).

[3] Thomas et al. (2000, 2008).

In traditional neoclassical growth theory, much attention has been given to the accumulation of physical and financial capital. In the endogenous growth models, more attention has been given to ideas, knowledge, and institutions, while physical capital has been put on a back burner. For poverty reduction, human (and social) capital and natural (and environmental) capital, such as land and water, are particularly important as these are the primary assets possessed by the poor.

The role of government in accumulating human capital and conserving natural capital is crucial. In many countries, there are market failures that lead to an underinvestment of human capital and overexploitation of natural capital. For example, the social returns from primary education and preventive health care are much higher than the private returns; therefore, the levels of investment in these public services would be suboptimal if the government fails to provide them.[4] There are also market failures in the form of undersupplying certain types of physical capital, such as rural roads, irrigation systems, or agricultural technology and innovation with some characteristics of public or semipublic goods, while overproducing pollution and greenhouse gas emissions that have negative externalities.

Government also plays a critical role in achieving a pattern of growth that is equitable and inclusive through equal opportunities, enhancing accumulation of human capital through equal access to basic health and education services, fiscal policies, and direct social assistance. In addition, government also plays a facilitating role in promoting economic growth by providing both hard and soft infrastructures, with the former including infrastructure investment and the latter research and development (R&D) and innovation, market information, and legal and regulatory framework to provide an inductive business climate (Li 2010).

1.2 The Growth Experience of China as a Case Study

The experience of three decades' rapid economic growth in China provides an important case study, illustrating how a narrow focus on the pace of growth without inadequate attention paid to the quality of growth can adversely affect development outcomes. China's fast economic growth is widely heralded as a growth miracle, with an annual GDP growth rate of 9.9 % over this period. Within a time span of three decades, from one of the poorest and most isolated countries in the world in 1979, with a per capita income of US$164, China became a well-established, middle-income country, with a per capita GDP US$ 6,819 (at constant 2005 international $). At the same time, more than 660 million people escaped poverty, based on the $1.25 per day poverty line. China overtook Japan as the world's second

[4] The term public good is often used to refer to goods that need to be supplied or at least be promoted by government because the private sector tends to undersupply them. This is due to the fact that a market is missing (such as with clean air) or there are severe market imperfections (such as preventive care or primary education) that prevent private firms from being paid enough to induce them to supply public goods at socially desirable levels.

largest economy and replaced Germany as the world's largest exporter of merchandise, with the trade to GDP ratio rising from 11.2 % in 1978 to 65 %—the highest among the world's large economies. The spectacular growth over the past three decades far exceeded the expectations of anyone at the outset of the transition, including Deng Xiaoping, the architect of China's reform and opening-up strategy (Lin 2010a).[5]

However, three decades' rapid growth has also transformed China from an egalitarian society into one of high inequality. The Gini coefficient reached 0.49 in 2008, from 0.31 in the early period of the reform, approaching the level of Latin American countries and surpassing all the countries in Europe. While the empirical relations between growth and inequality remain inconclusive since the pioneering work of Kuznet (1955), inequality can be distinguished between "good" inequality (incentive promoting) and "bad" (opportunity denying) inequality (World Bank 2009). In the case of China, not only is the level of inequality alarmingly high, much of China's recent increase in income inequality has been a result of unequal opportunities—excluding the majority population from the new employment opportunities that are more skill based as growth is driven by capital-intensive investment (Riskin 2010). The potential threat to political and social instability posed by growing inequality has now become a major policy concern in China.

Along with rising income inequality, disparities in social indicators, including health and education outcomes, are also on the rise. Gender equality, one of China's major pre-reform era achievements, has even reversed. The 2008 Millennium Development Goals Progress (UNDP) report highlights gender equity and equality as a key deficit for China during the country's economic boom and reform period.

Environmental sustainability, a critical aspect of the quality growth, has largely been sidelined, in growth-focused discourse on China. This is particularly reflected in the large and growing body of China-focused literature that is overwhelmingly devoted to China's growth miracle and its rising power in the global economy, while largely omitting the issue of environmental degradation and depletion of natural capital that is associated with its recent energy-intensive pattern of growth. China is now facing an environmental challenge on an unprecedented scale, with widespread environmental pollution posing a serious threat to human health and likely limiting future growth prospects. Some Chinese scholars argue that the country growth model is not sustainable because the pace of growth is largely based on the destruction of the ecological environment and the excessive use of resources, in addition to a rising income inequality (Zi 2011).[6]

While China represents one significant observation, evidence also highlights that a global economy based on current patterns of consumption and production is simply not sustainable. It is placing a heavy pressure on environment, resources, and the ecosystems on which our very livelihoods depend, and increasing the risk of global warming from excessive greenhouse gas emissions. The serious consequences of environmental and resource degradation, as well as the threat of global warming, both a result of economic expansion at great costs in the past, are a wake-up call to all of us.

---

[5] See full paper by Lin (2010b).

[6] See Zi (2011).

In 2009, leaders from 34 countries signed a Green Growth Declaration, affirming that they would strengthen their efforts to pursue green growth strategies as part of their responses to the environmental and climate change crisis, acknowledging that green and growth can go hand in hand (OECD 2009).[7] Green growth means fostering economic growth and development while ensuring that natural assets continue to provide the resources and environmental services on which our well-being relies (OECD 2011).[8] All of this highlights the urgency to focus on the quality of growth in formulating development policies for all countries, including both developed and developing ones.

1.3 Economic Growth as a Means to Development

In *Development as Freedom*, Sen (1990) emphasizes that development should be viewed as a process of expanding the real freedoms that people enjoy. Development must be focused on expanding individual entitlements, capabilities, freedom, and rights and economic growth is a means to development. Policymakers must reaffirm the development paradigm reshaped by Sen's research and critical thinking, not losing sight of broader development goals in the pursuit of growth. People should be both the beneficiaries of development and the agents of the progress and changes that development brings about. This requires economic development to be an inclusive process that benefits all individuals equitably and builds on the participation of each of them.

However, since 2008, development thinking has become less preoccupied with concerns about equity, environmental sustainability, conserving natural capital, and climate change and more inclined to stress the importance of growth. In a recent report on middle-income countries, Independent Evaluation Group (IEG) found that although many countries and the World Bank have been largely effective in the overarching priority of promoting growth and reducing poverty, they are much less effective in addressing rising inequality, governance and corruption, and environmental degradation. Country's success is almost exclusively defined by the rate of economic growth and growth policies, with inequality, environmental degradation, and depletion of natural resources largely omitted in the country performance assessment.

This preoccupation with the rate of growth is deep rooted in policymaking in many countries. It has recently been reinforced, no doubt, by the collapse of growth in developed economies and the spread of a global financial crisis and recessions (Mckinley 2010). But history teaches us that even in times of economic difficulties, one must not lose sight of the ultimate purpose of economic growth—improving well-being and prompting equity.

[7] See OECD (2009).

[8] See OECD (2011).

1.4 China's Rising Importance in the Global System

In the *Global Deal*, Stern (2008) highlights the two greatest problems of our time: overcoming poverty in the developing world and combating climate change. In addressing these two global problems, China has become a central player on the global stage. Despite the fact that hundreds of thousands of Chinese people have moved out of poverty, China is still home to about a fifth of the world's poor. Therefore, any progress achieved in poverty reduction in China will have a significant impact on global poverty.

In combating global warming, China is also playing a pivotal role. Although, since the mid-nineteenth century, about 30 % of total accumulated emissions have come from the United States and the developed world, many large emerging economies, such as China, India, and Brazil, have become significant emitters in recent years. China surpassed the United States to become the worlds' largest emitter of greenhouse gas in 2007, accounting for 8 % of total accumulated emissions. At the same time, China has also become the world's leading renewable energy producer as well as the biggest investor in renewable energy technologies. Since 2009, China has leapfrogged the West to emerge as the world's largest manufacturer of wind turbines and solar panels and is pushing equally hard to build nuclear reactors and the most efficient coal power plants to reduce carbon emissions.

We are living in an increasingly interdependent global system in which countries are connected through trade and investment, and the impact of economic activities of large countries, such as the United States, China, India, and Brazil, on environment and climate change is no longer confined within the national boundary. China, now the second largest economy in the world, should be particularly concerned about its quality of growth, because the economic and environmental benefits brought about by the improved quality of growth in China can have implications not only for the Chinese population but also for the rest of the world.

1.5 Policy Responses from China

Policymakers in China have responded to the challenges of rising inequality and environmental and resource degradation in earnest by setting a range of development targets and formulating new policies. In the 12th Five-Year Plan (FYP) for the period 2011–2015, the guiding principles are to promote inclusive growth to ensure that the benefits of economic growth are spread to a greater proportion of Chinese citizens. The key development objectives specified in the 12th FYP include rebalancing the economy through increasing domestic consumption while reducing capital-intensive investment and export, ameliorating social inequality, and protecting the environment. Fully aware of the serious consequences of rising inequality, the Chinese government places the issue of inequality high on its policy agenda—the CPC Central Committee convened the Development-Oriented Poverty Reduction

Working Meeting at its highest level in November 2011, officially releasing the *Outline for Development-Oriented Poverty Reduction for Rural China (2011–2020).*

The *outline* highlights that the main mission between 2011 and 2020 is to help people move out of poverty and improve their living standards more rapidly (the poverty line increased from 1,196 to 2,300 yuan at 2010 constant prices, which is equivalent to about US$1.8 per person per day based on 2005 PPP US$), improve ecological environment, enhance development capacity, and narrow development gaps. The Chinese government has also committed to making the utmost effort to promote a low-carbon economy and curb pollution, embarking on a path of green growth. Recently, Chinese Premier Wen Jiabao stated, "Green growth focuses on energy conservation, reduced energy consumption, sustainable development and environmental protection." Xi Jinping, President of the PRC, vowed that "Those who made rash decisions regardless of the ecological environment, resulting in serious consequences, must be brought to account, and should be held accountable for a lifetime. Only by implementing the strictest system and the most stringent rule of law can we provide reliable protection for ecological civilization."

1.6 Objectives and Scope of the Book

This book aims to provide compelling evidence based on most recent data sources to reshape current policy thinking on China's future economic growth and development by advocating a pattern of growth that should be equitable, inclusive, sustainable, and green. Countries differ in their structure of economic and political institutions, resource endowment, and history and cultural backgrounds, all of these factors playing a role in determining development outcomes. This China study also intends to provide some important lessons to many other developing countries seeking to promote economic growth and reduce poverty.

Using the quality growth framework, this book assesses China's three decades of economic growth, focusing on several key aspects of the growth process. These include sources of economic growth and structural transformation, poverty and income inequality, social disparities, the inclusiveness of the growth process, as well as the environmental costs, the energy intensity of production, and carbon emissions associated with China's pattern of growth. The assessment is carried out based primarily on evidence from the emerging large body of literature on China. However, the principal limitation of existing China-focused economic studies lies in its imbalances from the perspective of the quality growth concept, focusing mainly on growth accounting analysis and the impact of growth on poverty and inequality. Limited studies are devoted to structural transformation and China's structural imbalances, social disparities, and the role of science and technology on growth and productivity. Particularly lacking are studies that address the alarming environmental consequences of China's growth patterns within an overall quality growth framework.

This book contributes to the economic growth and development literature and current policy discourse on China by broadening the policy analysis in several important new areas using the most recent data available. These include (1) analyzing macroeconomic factors that underlie the need for China to advance economic transformation; (2) examining how social inequality, including health, education, and gender, has evolved; and (3) presenting the scale of environmental problems associated with China's growth miracle. This book represents the first attempt to integrate the issue of environmental sustainability and climate change in the quality growth context, providing readers with a comprehensive account of China's success and challenges in its three decades' fast economic growth.

This book is organized as follows. Chapter 1 discusses China's miracle in economic growth and poverty reduction; Chap. 2 explains how China has succeed in sustaining a high growth rate and poverty alleviation for three decades; Chap. 3 explains why China must advance economic transformation and improve the quality of growth; Chap. 4 assesses the impact of economic growth on inequality; Chap. 5 focuses on social outcomes, including health, education, and gender equality; Chap. 6 presents the scale of the environmental and resource degradation as well as its energy use under the current production pattern; and the Conclusion concludes.

References

Chandra V, Lin JY, Wang Y (2013) Leading Dragon phenomenon: new opportunities for catch-up in low-income countries. Asian Dev Rev 30(1):52–84

Christiaensen LJ, Demery L, Kühl J (2006) The role of agriculture in poverty reduction: an empirical perspective. The World Bank, Washington, DC

IEG (2007a) Annual review of development effectiveness. Independent Evaluation Group. World Bank Publication, Washington, DC

IEG (2007b) Development results in middle-income countries. An evaluation of the World Bank's support. Report no. 39962, 8 June 2007. Independent Evaluation Group. World Bank, Washington, DC

Kuznet S (1955) Economic growth and income inequality. Am Econ Rev 65:1–28

Li C (2010) "China's consumption myth", Hong Kong Monetary Authority working paper. Presentation at the PBoC/IMF workshop of "Catalyzing Domestic Demand", Beijing, 21 Jan 2010

Lin JY (2010a) New structural economics. World Bank policy research working paper 5197. World Bank, Washington, DC

Lin JY (2010b) The China miracle demystified. Paper prepared for the panel on 'Perspectives on Chinese Economic Growth' at the Econometric Society World Congress, Shanghai, 19 Aug 2010

Loayza N, Raddatz C (2006) The composition of growth matters for poverty alleviation. World Bank policy research working paper 4077. World Bank, Washington, DC

Maddison A (2010) Is a large database widely utilized by economist. He pass away in 2010. See http://www.ggdc.net/maddison/maddison-project/home.htm

Mckingley T (2010) Revisiting the dynamics of growth, inequality and poverty reduction. Centre for Development Policy & Research, School of Oriental & African Studies, University of London, London

Montalvo JG, Ravallion M (2010) The pattern of growth and poverty reduction in China. J Comp Econ 38(1):2–16

OECD (2009) Declare on green growth. Organisation for Economic Co-operation and Development, Paris

OECD (2011) Towards green growth. Organisation for Economic Co-operation and Development, Paris

Ravallion M, Chen S (2004) China's (uneven) progress against poverty. World Bank policy research working paper no. WPS 3408. World Bank, Washington, DC

Riskin C (2010) Inequality and economic crisis in China. In: Banerjee L, Dasgupta A, Islam R (eds) Development, equity and poverty. Macmillan Publishers India Ltd, Gurgaon

Sen A (1990) Gender and cooperative con. icts. In: Tinker I (ed) Persistent inequalities: women and world development. Oxford University Press, New York

Stern N (2008) The global deal: climate change and the creation of a new era of progress and prosperity. Public Affairs, New York

Thomas V, Dailami M, Dhareshwar A, López RE, Kaufmann D, Kishor N, Wang Y (2000) The quality of growth. Oxford University Press, New York

Thomas V, López RE, Wang Y (2008) Fiscal policies for the quality of growth. IEG briefing 9, The World Bank, Washington, DC

World Bank (2005) Pro-poor growth in the 1990s: lessons and Insights from 14 Countries. Operationalizing pro-poor growth research program. World Bank, Washington, DC

World Bank (2009) Addressing China's water scarcity: recommendations for selected water resource management issues. World Bank, Washington, DC

Zi Z (2011) Gan shi you si (感时忧世). Guangxi Normal University Publishing House, Nanning

Chapter 2
China's Miracle in Growth and Poverty Reduction

Since China started its economic reform program in 1978, the country has created two miracles in modern history. First, China has transformed itself from one of the poorest countries in the world to a middle-income one within a span of three decades through sustained economic growth at a record pace. In the 1980s and 1990s, China was a major aid recipient among developing countries. From the beginning of the twenty-first century, however, it has become a major donor to Africa, Latin America, and Southeast Asia.[1] China's rising economic power comes from its growth miracle—a rapid and sustained high growth rate over three decades.

The second miracle is on poverty reduction. China has made the largest contribution to the reduction of global poverty by lifting over a fifth of the world's poor people out of poverty. Based on the World Bank international poverty line of $1.25 per person per day, the number of poor people dropped from 842 million to 166 million in China during the past three decades—more than 600 million people had moved out of poverty.[2] This is equivalent to lifting more than half of the population of the entire African continent out of poverty. This chapter provides an overview of China's economic growth miracle and its success in improving living standards of the rural population over the past three decades.

---

[1] In 2007, China provided about $1.4 billion Oversea Development Aid (ODA) to Africa, whereas ODA to Africa from the United States amounted to $7.6 billion and from the EU, $6 billion (Brautigam 2011).

[2] According to World Bank estimates, the people below the poverty line of $1.25 per person per day in consumption accounted for 12.6 % of the total population in 2008.

X. Wang et al., *The Quality of Growth and Poverty Reduction in China*,
International Research on Poverty Reduction, DOI 10.1007/978-3-642-36346-7_2,

2.1 China's Economic Miracle

2.1.1 *Unprecedented Growth Record*

From 1978 to 2010, per capita GDP in China rose 16 times, from a level of about \$150 (in 2000 constant US\$) in the 1970s to about \$2423 in 2010 through sustained high growth. China saw an average annual GDP growth rate of about 10 % for three decades. Both the duration and the rate of growth outperformed all major large economies in the world as shown in Fig. 2.1. China's growth record also surpassed the East Asian miracles of Taiwan, Hong Kong, Singapore, and Korea in the 1980s and 1990s which grew at a rate of about 7–8 % for less than two decades.

The comparison of China and India (Fig. 2.2), two countries that were comparable in terms of population size and stage of development, is particularly striking. In the early 1980s, both countries were at the same level of income, but three decades later, per capita income in China was nearly three times that of India in 2009.

After the global financial crisis in 2008, while many countries experienced an economic downturn, China remained resilient to the economic shocks. The growth rate kept at 10.3 % in 2010 and GDP reached 39.7983 trillion yuan (equivalent to \$5.8791 trillion). China became the world's second largest economy in 2010, second only to the United States (National Bureau of Statistics 2010).

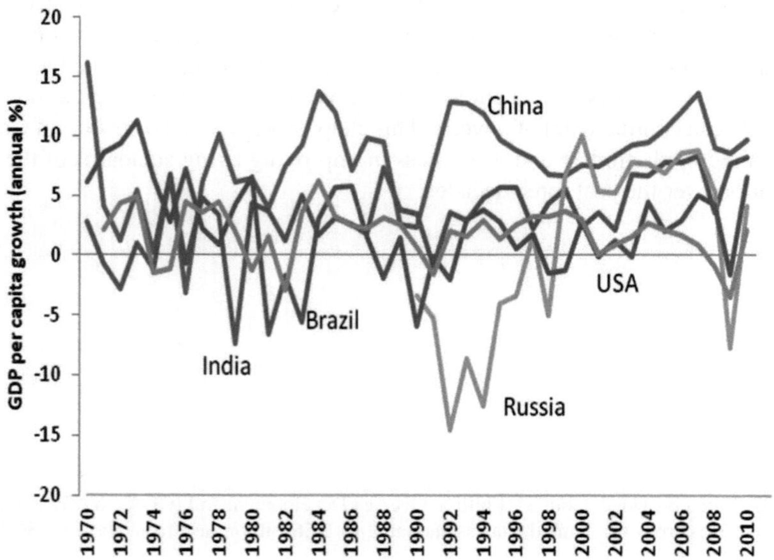

Fig. 2.1 GDP growth rate (*Source*: Author's own construction based on China Statistical Yearbooks)

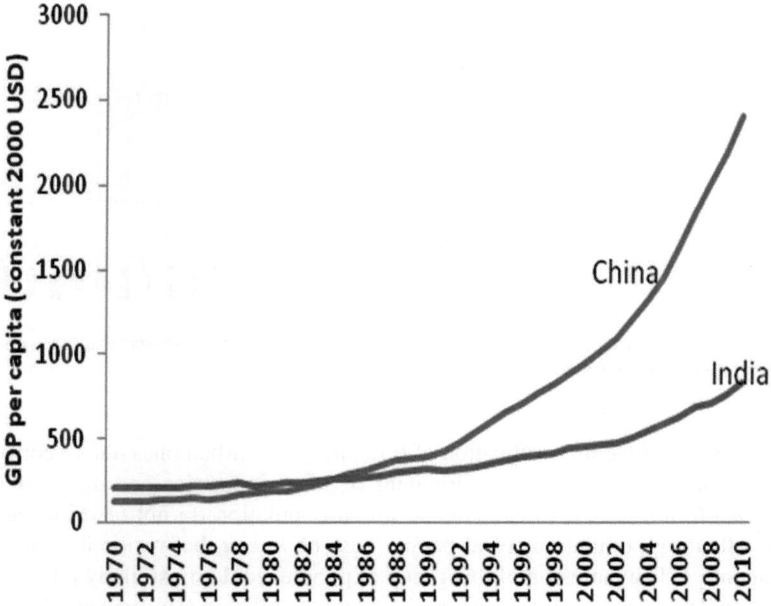

Fig. 2.2 GDP per capita: China and India (*Source*: Author's own construction based on China Statistical Yearbooks)

2.1.2 *Rapid Structural Transformation and Urbanization*

The three decades' rapid economic growth has also been accompanied by fundamental transformation of the economic structure. China has transformed from a low productive agriculture-based economy to one that is characterized by a coordinated development of the primary (agriculture), secondary (industry), and tertiary (services) sectors. The GDP share of the value added of primary, secondary, and tertiary industries has changed from 28 %, 48 %, and 24 % in 1978 to 10 %, 47 %, and 43 %, respectively, in 2010 (Fig. 2.3). The foundational role of agriculture in the economy has been continuously strengthened through improvement in productivity—the output per capita in the agricultural sector increased from 106 yuan in 1978 to 3,022 yuan in 2010 and grain production increased from 304.8 million tons in 1978 to 528.5 million tons in 2008 (National Bureau of Statistics 2010).

During this period of time, a large-scale population relocation also took place across sectors and between urban and rural areas. The share of employment in agriculture dropped from 78 % in 1978 to only 40 % in 2010 (Fig. 2.3), releasing a large amount of surplus labor that made it possible to expand industrial and services sectors at record speeds. At the same time, China also saw rapid urbanization. Despite the official household registration system (*hukou*) which was designed to restrict rural migration to cities, China's urban population has increased by threefold, rising from 17 % in 1970 to over 45 % in 2010. This increase in urban population is

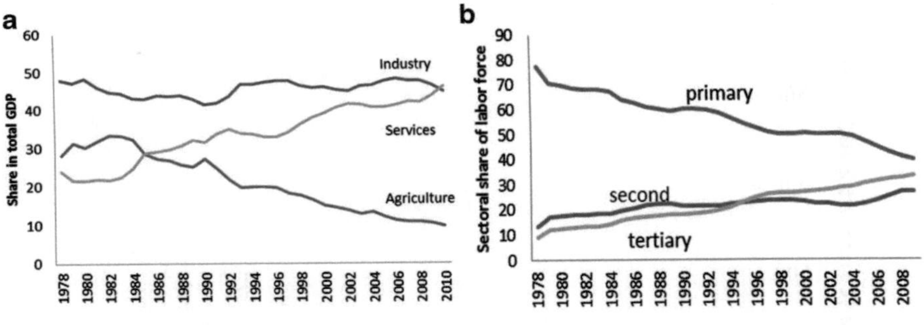

Fig. 2.3 Sectoral share of (**a**) GDP and (**b**) labor force: 1978–2010 (*Source*: Authors' own construction based on China Statistical Yearbooks)

largely a result of the reclassification of rural areas into urban ones due to conversion of agricultural land for the development of local industries and services sector (Biller 2006). Official estimates of the urban population do not take into account China's floating population (rural people with no *hukou*, but reside in cities semi-permanently). The inclusion of this group of people would most likely push China's urban population well over half the total national population (Hofman and Wu 2008).

China's structural transformation, in many respects, resembled closely the process of industrialization that took place in Europe in the eighteenth and nineteenth centuries, in the United States in the early twentieth century, and in the Newly Industrialized Economies in East Asia in the 1970s and 1980s. However, it took much less time for China, a country with nearly a quarter of the world population, to complete the transformation from an agriculture-based economy to one dominated by industry and services sectors. With the economic growth, China's exports structure has also changed from primary goods—led pattern to machinery and transport equipment led (Fig. 2.4).

2.1.3 Leading World Trader and FDI Destination

In the 1970s, China was a much closed economy—total value of China's import and export was only $20.6 billion, ranking 32nd in the world trade and accounting for less than 1 % of the world's total trade. Within three decades, China became the world's largest exporter and second largest importer. In 2010 the total value of China's import and export reached $2.974 trillion, 144 times as much as that in 1978, with the total volumes of China's export and import accounting for 10.4 % and 9.1 % of the world's total, respectively.

The structure of trade is a good indicator of structural transformation: as late as 1984, China was an exporter of resource and primary products. Fifty percent of export comprised of crude oil, crude coal, and animal and agricultural products. Along with the opening of trade and FDI, China established several special economic

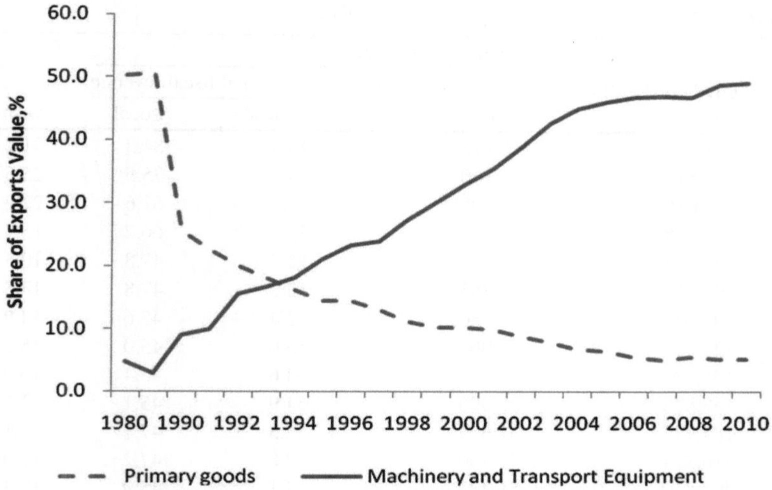

Fig. 2.4 China's export structure (*Source*: China Statistical Yearbook 2011)

zones, started learning by doing and learning by exporting, structural of export upgraded in three steps, first from primary products to low-end labor-intensive textile, clothing, and toys in the 1990s and then to medium range but labor-intensive products including auto parts, machinery, and equipment, and since 2001, China has joined the WTO and become an integral part of the global supply chains, producing a wide range of manufactured products (see Fig. 2.4).

China also became a major destination of FDI. According to official statistics, FDI was near zero in the late 1970s and rose to about only \$2.3 billion in 1984–1989. Since the early 1990s, China has become the largest FDI recipient among developing countries. In 2009, FDI inflow to China reached \$95 billion, accounting for about 19.9 % of total FDI in developing countries and 8.5 % of total global FDI (UNCADT 2011).

2.1.4 Strong Fiscal Capacity and Foreign Exchange Reserve

China's economic growth has also strengthened its national fiscal capacity and foreign exchange reserve. State revenue doubled between 1978 and 1985, rising from only 113.2 billion yuan in 1978 to 200.5 billion yuan in 1985. Since 1995, government revenue has witnessed even faster growth, amounting to 8.308 trillion yuan in 2010, with an average annual growth rate of 14.4 % (at current prices) as shown in Table 2.1.

The increased government revenue has provided the government with the capacity to sustain economic development and respond effectively to various economic and financial crises as well as to natural disasters. From 1978 to 2010, the total volume

Table 2.1 GDP and fiscal revenue in China (1978–2010)

	GDP (100 million yuan)	Total fiscal revenue			
		Value (100 million yuan)	% of total fiscal revenue		% of GDP
			Central	Local	
1978	3,645	1,132	15.5	84.5	31.1
1980	4,546	1,160	24.5	75.5	25.5
1985	9,016	2,005	38.4	61.6	22.2
1990	18,668	2,937	33.8	66.2	15.7
1995	60,794	6,242	52.2	47.8	10.3
2000	99,215	13,395	52.2	47.8	13.5
2001	109,655	16,386	52.4	47.6	14.9
2002	120,333	18,904	55.0	45.0	15.7
2003	135,823	21,715	54.6	45.4	16.0
2004	159,878	26,396	54.9	45.1	16.5
2005	184,937	31,649	52.3	47.7	17.1
2006	216,314	38,760	52.8	47.2	17.9
2007	265,810	51,322	54.1	45.9	19.3
2008	314,045	61,330	53.3	46.7	19.5
2009	340,903	68,518	52.4	47.6	20.1
2010	397,983	83,080	51.1	48.9	20.9

Source: CEIC, authors' estimates

of fiscal expenditure rose from 112 billion yuan to 8,987 billion yuan, with an annual rate of increase of 14.7 % (at current prices). The major areas of government spending included improving social services such as education and health care, access to safe water and sanitation services, and financing public goods, such as research and development, innovation, and infrastructure upgrading.

China has transformed from a country with a severe foreign exchange shortage to one with the largest reserve in the world. In 1978, China's foreign exchange reserve was only $167 million, only $0.17 per capita (equivalent to less than 1 yuan) which seriously limited the country's ability to import high-technology commodities crucial for modernizing the economy. Since the early 1990s, the foreign exchange reserves have been continuously increasing over time: in 1990, China's foreign exchange reserves reached $11.1 billion; in 1996, the figure exceeded a hundred billion US dollars, soaring to $105 billion; in 2006, the reserves exceeded one trillion US dollars, reaching $1.0663 trillion, higher than that in Japan, ranking first in the world; and in 2010, China's foreign exchange reserves rose to $2.8473 trillion (China National Bureau of Statistics 2011).

No doubt, three decades of economic growth have transformed China from a poor agriculture-based economy to one dominated by industrial and services sectors, with per capita income reaching the level of middle-income countries. As China's role in the world economy has become dominant in terms of trade and FDI inflow, its fiscal capacity and foreign exchange reserves also have been strengthened significantly. China is now widely heralded as the new rising economic power, joining the ranks with the United States and other major economies in the world.

2.2 Major Achievements in Rural Poverty Reduction

2.2.1 Sharp Decline in Income Poverty

Along with fast growth, China also saw the biggest success in poverty alleviation in history. Poverty was predominantly a rural phenomenon. Three decades' economic reform and growth has improved the living standards of the vast Chinese rural population, through a continuous increase in food production, improvement in rural infrastructure, and employment opportunities generated in both the fast-growing rural industries and the urban areas as rural–urban migration became a dominant force of economic transformation.

Based on China's official poverty line, the poor population was reduced from 250 million in 1978 to 26.88 million in 2010, and the proportion of poor people in the total rural population dropped from 30.7 to 2.8 %. Lifting such a large number of people out of poverty in such a short time span is unprecedented in human history. The 2009 World Bank report, "Assessment of Poverty and Inequality in China," also confirms that China has made more significant achievements in poverty reduction based on the World Bank poverty line of $1.08 per person per day (1993 PPP US$), which is equivalent to about 888 yuan per person per year in 2003 rural prices. According to the recent estimation based on the World Bank poverty line of $1.25 per person per day (2005 PPP US$), China has a more significant achievement of poverty reduction.

During this period, the number of poor in all developing countries dropped from 1.5 billion to 1.1 billion, the majority of them from China. Indeed, China's poverty alleviation efforts in the last two decades of the twentieth century made a significant impact on reducing the number of poor people in developing countries (World Bank 2009; Haughton and Khandker 2009).

2.2.2 Increased Household Ownership of Durable Goods

With the continuous improvement of farmers' income and declining poverty, the majority of rural residents can gradually purchase consumer durable goods to improve their quality of life. The increase in household durable goods ownership provides another indicator of welfare improvement of the rural population, which is a more comprehensive and robust measure of living standards than incomes. As shown in Fig. 2.5, the ownership of a range of consumer durables in rural China, including key counties with the high poverty rates,[3] increased sharply between 2002 and 2010.

[3] In 2000, 529 counties with the high poverty rate were identified as key counties to receive government-led development-oriented antipoverty programs and financial assistance to support their efforts to move out of poverty.

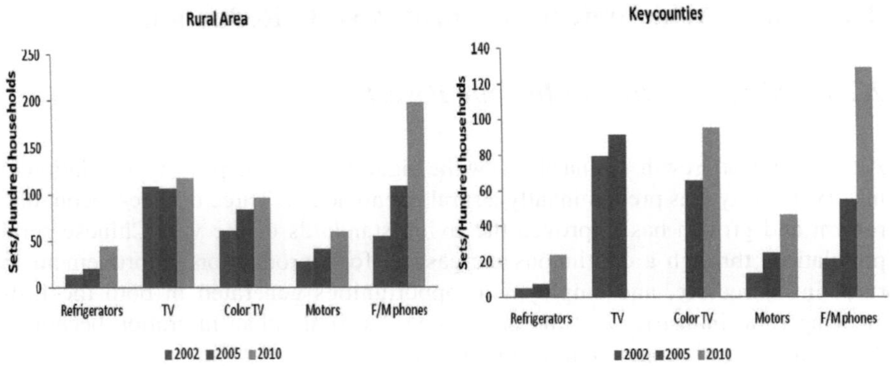

Fig. 2.5 Household ownership of consumer durables in rural China (*Source:* Poverty Monitoring Report of Rural China 2010. *Note*: In 2001, 592 counties with high poverty incidence were identified as the key counties for receiving antipoverty programs and development assistance)

2.2.3 Improvement in Health and Education

The Chinese government also launched a series of health and education programs targeted at children from poor households. These include the nine-year compulsory education, the "free tuition," "free textbooks," and "living allowance for boarding students from poor families," "Project Hope," and other policies and programs (see Box 2.1). Children from the key counties have particularly benefited from these targeted programs. According to the National Rural Household Survey, by the end of 2010, the schooling rate of children aged 7–15 in China had reached 98.0 %, increasing by 3.9 percentage points from 2002, while children of the same age group from the key counties reached almost the same level of the national rural population (97.7 %), increasing 6.6 percentage points from 2002 (Fig. 2.6).

The overall health status of the key county rural population has also improved between 2002 and 2010 (Table 2.2). The proportion of healthy people in key counties was above 93 %, while other health indicators such as proportion of people with disabilities or suffering from serious illness/chronic illness all declined slightly. In addition, the proportion of the people who could afford medical treatment rose from 83.8 % in 2002 to 91.4 % in 2010.

2.2.4 Major Phases of Progress in Poverty Reduction

Although China has achieved the most success in poverty reduction globally, progress has been uneven over time and across regions (Chen and Ravallion 2007). The progress was far greater in the early 1980s and the mid-1990s, slowed down beginning in the late 1990s as shown in Fig. 2.10. The coastal regions saw a much larger reduction in poverty than inland areas. This was largely an outcome of a combination

Box 2.1: Special Projects and Funds for Basic Education

In order to achieve universal compulsory education and promote equal access to education for children in poverty-stricken areas, the central government has earmarked specific transfer payments to these areas, in particular in western China, through a series of programs and projects.

Compulsory education project in poverty-stricken areas: In 1994, the Financial Department of the National Commission of Education and Culture and Education Department of the Ministry of Finance completed a survey of compulsory education in Shanxi and Inner Mongolia and made a proposal for a compulsory education project in poverty-stricken areas. This is the project with the highest level of financial resources and the most extensive coverage for the promotion of compulsory education in poverty-stricken areas. During the first stage of this project (1995–2000), a total of 12.6 billion yuan was committed, including 3.9 billion yuan from the central government and 8.8 billion yuan from lower-level governments. From 1995 to 1997, 383 poor counties in the central and western regions received assistance, and from 1998 to 2000, assistance was directed to 469 poor counties in the western region. From 2001 to 2005, the central government continued its efforts by implementing the second stage of this project, which focused on poverty-stricken areas and ethnic minority areas. A total of 7.36 billion yuan was committed, including 5 billion yuan from the central government and 2.35 billion yuan from subnational governments. The government launched a third stage in 2006, which aims to achieve the goal of universal compulsory nine-year education by 2010.

Project for renovating dilapidated rural primary school and middle school buildings: In order to improve school conditions in rural areas, the central government decided to implement a project for renovating dilapidated buildings of rural primary and middle schools from 2001, with the main focus on renovating buildings whose load-bearing structure could not sustain normal use and posed safety threats ("D-level" dilapidated buildings). During the first stage, from 2001 to 2002, the central and provincial governments invested a total of 5.2 billion yuan, of which 3 billion yuan was committed by the central government (mainly through the issuance of treasury bonds) and 17 million square meters of dilapidated school buildings was renovated. Since 2003, the government has committed to continue the implementation of this project.

"Two frees and one subsidy": In order to overcome the financial barriers to access to compulsory education in rural areas and in particular to make boarding an affordable option for poor families, the central government launched a new policy in 2004 to provide student from poor families in poverty-stricken rural areas in western China with free textbooks, to exempt them from paying miscellaneous fees, and to grant living allowances to boarding students. This was extended in 2005 to all 592 rural counties officially designated as poverty stricken. In 2006, all miscellaneous fees for compulsory education in rural areas in western China were abolished, and this policy was extended to central and eastern China in 2007.

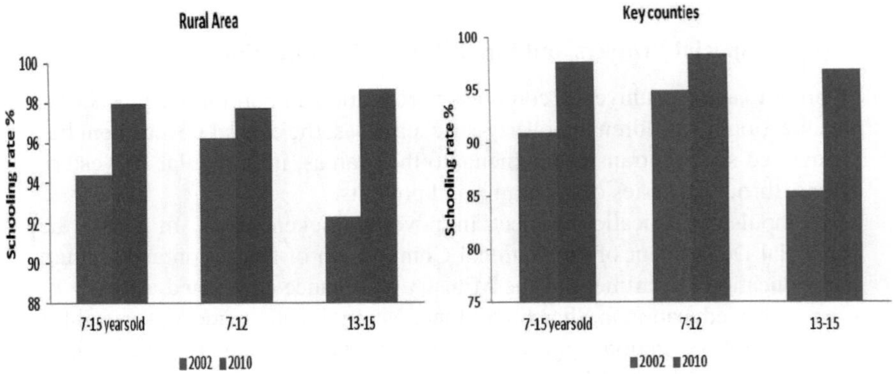

Fig. 2.6 School enrollment of children in rural China (%) (*Source:* Poverty Monitoring Report of Rural China 2010)

Table 2.2 Health of rural residents in key poverty counties (%)

Year	Healthy	Disabled	Suffer from serious illness	Suffer from chronic illness	Sickly	Proportion of the people who could afford medical treatment
2002	91.7	1.4	0.6	2	4.3	83.8
2003	92.8	1.2	0.5	1.6	3.8	85.3
2004	93.0	1.2	0.5	1.6	3.8	85.2
2005	93.3	1	0.4	1.6	3.7	86.1
2006	93.2	1.1	0.4	1.5	3.8	86.5
2007	93.2	1.1	0.4	1.5	3.8	88.6
2008	93.3	1	0.4	1.4	3.8	90.1
2009	92.9	1.3	0.4	1.5	3.9	91.2
2010	93.1	1.2	0.4	1.4	3.8	91.4

Source: Poverty Monitoring Report of Rural China 2010

of different economic growth patterns, government investment in rural development (infrastructure and social services), and the effectiveness of government-led antipoverty development programs. The progress in poverty reduction is summarized in three major phases marked by the introduction of key reform policies and antipoverty programs.

Phase I: 1978–1985, large-scale poverty alleviation was made possible by rural institutional reforms. During this period, the Chinese government initiated the rural household land contract system which provides rural households with equal land access, liberalized agriculture markets and prices, and provided policy support to foster the development of rural nonfarming sectors, such as township and village enterprises (TVEs). These reforms led to a sharp increase in agriculture production and increase in rural household incomes. The increased food availability, and income from diversified economic activities, played an instrumental role in safeguarding the rural population from poverty in the form of hunger and malnutrition which was prevalent in rural areas before 1978. The number of poverty-stricken people dropped from 250 million in 1978 to 125 million in 1985, with an average annual decline of 17.86 million, and the poverty incidence fell from 30.7 to 14.8 %, with an average annual decline of 9.4 %.

Phase II: 1986–2000, targeted development-oriented poverty alleviation program. During the period of 1985–1993, the progress in rural poverty reduction remained stagnant and rural income increased at a much slower rate, mainly due to stagnation of agricultural production after the impact of initial reforms diminished. The number of poor people in fact increased from 89 million in 1984 to 103 million in 1989 (Fan 2007). Since 1989, along with policies that supported rural economic diversification, gradual allowance of labor migration, government also introduced regionally targeted development-oriented poverty alleviation programs. In 2000, the number of people below the national poverty line was reduced to 94.22 million and the incidence of poverty dropped to 10.2 %.

Phase III: 2001–2010, government program to achieve the goal of building a moderately prosperous society, WTO accession, and abolishment of agricultural tax. At this stage, the Chinese government promulgated and implemented the "China Rural Poverty Alleviation and Development Program (2001–2010)," which clearly put forward the goal of meeting the basic living needs (food and clothing) for the remaining poor people before 2010 as a national policy priority. In 2004, the government abolished the agricultural tax. The government's strategy of building a moderately prosperous society has focused on promoting the development of poor areas and targeting poor people, with the identification of 592 counties with high poverty incidence as the key counties for receiving antipoverty programs and development assistance.

Since China joined the WTO in 2000, poverty reduction resumed at a rapid rate, with the poverty headcount index reduced by a third within 3 years (Dollar 2007). During phase III, the number of poor people was reduced from 90.30 million in 2001 to 26.88 million in 2010, and the incidence of poverty fell from 9.8 to 2.8 % (Table 2.2). Among the 592 key counties, the poverty incidence fell from 24.3 % in 2002 to 8.3 % in 2010.

2.2.5 Poverty Reduction Progress in the 592 Key Counties

In assessing China's success in rural poverty reduction, it is important to focus on the progress made in rural households residing in the 592 key counties where government-led antipoverty programs were implemented. Rigorous assessment of the effectiveness of these programs requires properly designed impact evaluation studies of China's Rural Poverty Alleviation and Development Program. In the absence of impact studies, a comparison of improvement of living standards among rural households in key counties with national rural averages can provide useful insight into program effectiveness. Table 2.3 shows clearly that poverty incidence

Table 2.3 Rural poverty: 2000–2010

		Nationwide		Key counties	
Year	Poverty line (yuan per person per year)	Poor people (10,000)	Poverty incidence %	Poor people (10,000)	Poverty incidence %
2000	865	9,422	10.2		
2001	872	9,030	9.8		
2002	869	8,645	9.2	4,828	24.3
2003	882	8,517	9.1	4,706	23.7
2004	924	7,587	8.2	4,193	21.0
2005	944	6,432	6.8	3,611	18.0
2006	958	5,698	6.0	3,110	15.4
2007	1,067	4,320	4.6	2,620	13.0
2008	1,196	4,007	4.2	2,421	11.9
2009	1,196	3,597	3.6	2,175	10.7
2010	1,274	2,688	2.8	1,693	8.3

Source: Poverty Monitoring Report of Rural China 2010

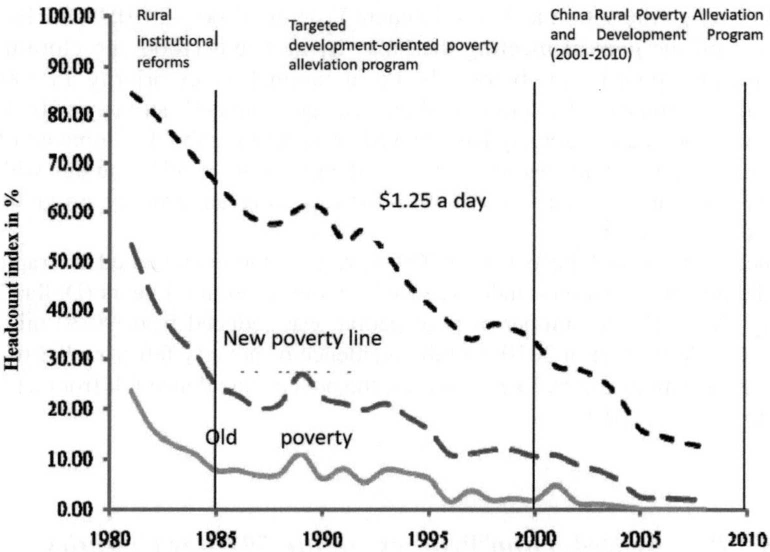

Fig. 2.7 Major policy/program changes in China (1978–2011) (*Source:* Author edit based on Chen (2011), Lecture at IPRCC)

in key counties declined much faster than the national average between 2002 and 2010. Other indicators, such as the larger increase in household durable goods ownership (Fig. 2.6) and in children's schooling rate between 2002 and 2010 (Fig. 2.7), also provide supportive evidence of the success of the geographically targeted development programs implemented in the key counties during the third phase.

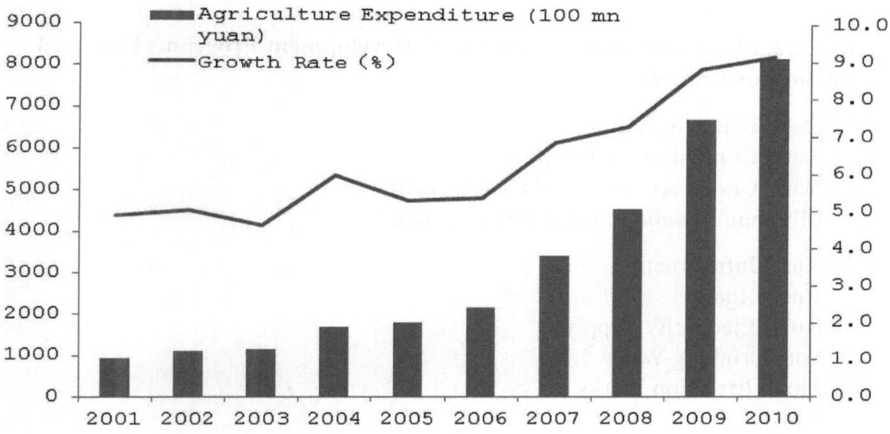

Fig. 2.8 Fiscal expenditure in agricultural and rural development (*Data Source*: Finance Yearbook of China 2010)

2.2.6 Improvement in Rural Infrastructure

Increased fiscal capacity, as a result of the GDP increase, has boosted government spending in agricultural and rural development (Fig. 2.8). Government spending has focused in production-enhancing rural investment, such as agriculture R&D and irrigation, rural education, and infrastructure, all contributing to agricultural growth and reducing rural poverty in China (see Box 2.2). Indeed, Fan (2007) shows government spending in rural education had the largest impact in reducing poverty, followed by agricultural R&D and investment in rural roads.

In the third phase of rural development, the strategic framework of poverty reduction was developed based on the idea of "integrated village development." The poverty alleviation and development program has emphasized the development capacity of poverty-stricken villages to enable poor people to earn their way out of poverty. These programs focused on improving rural roads, access to electricity, access to telephones, and access to TVs, the so-called "four accesses" project, to address poverty. Figure 2.9 shows that the proportion of "four accesses" in the key counties has been significantly improved since 2002. By 2010, 88.1 % of the villages located in the key counties had access to high-speed roads, 98.0 % of the villages had access to electricity, 92.9 % had access to telephones, and 95.6 % had access to TV programs.

The Chinese government also devoted special funds to improve safe drinking water for households in key counties. Water contamination has been a major source of dysentery and other infectious diseases in poor rural areas. As a result of targeted interventions that are part of the antipoverty programs, the proportion of the contaminated drinking water sources in key counties dropped from 15.5 % in 2002 to 5.8 % in 2009, and the proportion of rural households with no access to drinking water dropped from 19.8 % in 2002 to 9.5 % in 2009 (Fig. 2.10).

Box 2.2: Major Agricultural and Rural Development Programs Financed by the Government

1. Rural Public Services
   Rural Compulsory Education
   Rural Cooperative Medical Care System
   Minimum Livelihood Guarantee System
2. Rural Infrastructure
   Rural Roads
   Rural Electricity Supply
   Safe Drinking Water
   Small Irrigation Works
   Biogas
3. Support Agricultural Production
   Comprehensive Agricultural Development Projects
   Agricultural Cooperatives
   Modern agriculture demonstration project
4. Subsidies to Farmers
   Sloping Land Conversion Programme (SLCP)
   Forest Ecological Compensation Fund (FECF)
   Grain, Pork and Cow Subsidy
   Agricultural Machinery Subsidy
   Agricultural Capital Goods Subsidy
5. Earmark of Poverty Reduction
   Agricultural Industrialization
   Migration
   Training for Rural Migrant Workers
   Village-based Integrated Development Projects

   By author's classification

2.3 An International Perspective and Lessons from China

2.3.1 A Comparative Perspective

It is useful to assess China's poverty reduction progress from an international perspective. In a comparative study of three large emerging economies as shown in Fig. 2.11, China, Brazil, and India, Chen and Ravallion (2007) provide important insights into key factors that are associated with country's success in reducing poverty.

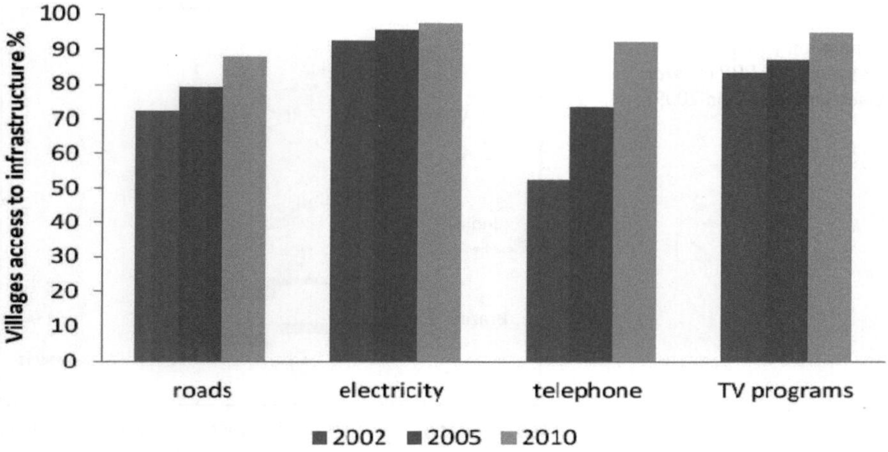

Fig. 2.9 Infrastructure development in natural villages in key counties (*Source*: Poverty Monitoring Report of Rural China 2010)

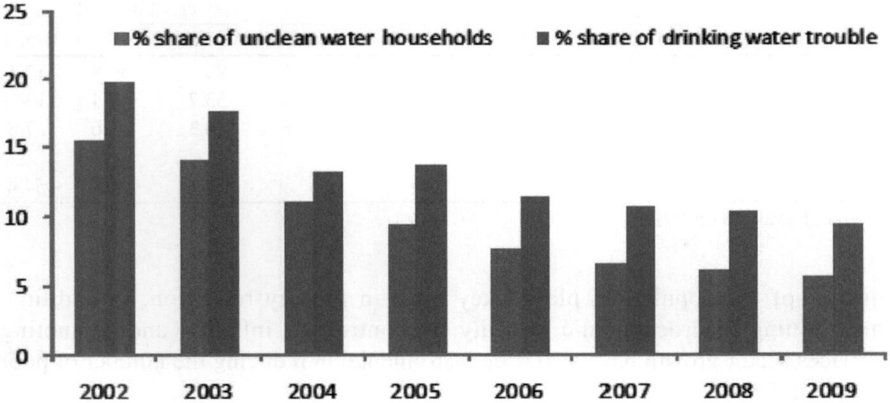

Fig. 2.10 Drinking water conditions of rural households in key counties (*Source:* Author's calculations)

Table 2.4 summarizes changes in key indicators for the three countries over the period of 1981–2005. During this period, the three large economies experienced a starkly different growth rate, with China achieving 8.8 % GDP per capita growth, while Brazil and India maintained 0.8 % and 3.9 %, respectively. In the case of Brazil, despite the relatively slow growth and high level of inequality, it managed to reduce poverty (measured by poverty head index) by 54 % between 1981 and 2005 while keeping inequality from rising. The implementation of reforms to the social security system and the introduction of large-scale social assistance transfer programs, including various conditional transfer programs that covered over one

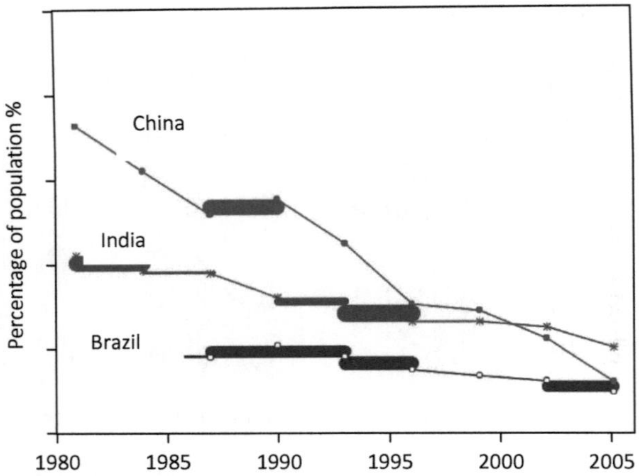

Fig. 2.11 Percentage of population living below $1.25 a day at 2005 PPP (*Source*: Chen and Ravallion 2009)

Table 2.4 Comparison of China, India, and Brazil

	GDP per capita ($PPP per year)			Gini index (%)			Poverty headcount index (poverty line $1.25)		
	China	India	Brazil	China	India	Brazil	China	India	Brazil
1981	543	901	7,072	29.1	35.1	57.5	84	59.8	17.1
1993	1,505	1,274	7,241	35.5	30.8	59.7	53.7	49.4	13
2005	4,076	2,233	8,471	41.5	33.4	57.6	16.3	41.6	7.8
1981–2005									
Change %	8.8	3.9	0.8				−80.6	−30.4	−54.4

Source: Ravallion (2009)

quarter of the population, played key roles in poverty reduction. In addition, maintaining macroeconomic stability by controlling inflation and promoting services sector growth have also been instrumental in reducing the number of poor people in Brazil.

India provides a middle case in terms of growth, with a rate much faster than that of Brazil but smaller than that of China. Growth was largely driven by the services sector in IT, software, and financial services, which require high-skills and education attainment. Such a growth pattern has brought moderate reduction in poverty, about 30 % reduction between 1981 and 2005, partially due to its high inequality in human capital and land access that are deeply rooted in its caste system and long history of social inequality.

In comparison with India and Brazil, China experienced the highest growth among the three countries and also saw the largest reduction in the headcount index by 81 %. One striking feature in China is the sharp rising inequality, in contrast with Brazil and India. Indeed, it was the rapid economic growth—particularly, the sectoral pattern of growth in the first two decades of reform, equal access to land among rural residents, as well as low inequality in human capital in the initial stage of economic transition—that provided the foundation for China's success in both generating growth and reducing poverty on a massive scale.

2.3.2 Lessons from China's Poverty Reduction Experience

The speed and scale of rural poverty reduction in China are indeed unprecedented in human history, and the Chinese experience can offer important lessons to other developing countries in their efforts to eradicate poverty. While the economic growth brought by reform programs and sound macroeconomic policies is instrumental in lifting many people out of poverty, the proactive role of government in both supporting rural development and financing investment and implementing targeted development-oriented poverty reduction programs is equally critical in poverty reduction.

The rural household contract system introduced in 1978, one of the major institutional reforms in China, provided the rural population with the most fundamental economic rights to enable them to exercise the freedom of making economic choices to earn their way out of poverty. The allowance of expanding nonfarm activities (i.e., rural enterprises) and gradual allowance of population migration within China further expanded the rural population's freedom and capacity to diversify economic activities to increase incomes and improve living standards.

While the transition from a centrally controlled system to a market economy provides the opportunity for individuals to make economic decisions based on price signals, government investment in areas where market fails is critical in improving agricultural productivity. For example, the government has invested heavily in advancing agricultural technological innovation and adoption and in rural infrastructure investment, which has been critical in raising agricultural productivity, as reflected by the manyfold increase in food production.

To achieve freedom from poverty, economic empowerment in the forms of land entitlements and making economic choices must be combined with human capabilities, including basic education attainment and good health. China's large-scale government-led rural poverty alleviation programs that focus on developing both human capacities (health and education) and other rural infrastructure and technology innovation are some of the important driving forces in reducing rural poverty. The success in improving the living standards in the 592 key poverty-stricken counties provides a good illustration of the impact of development-oriented poverty alleviation program on rural poverty.

The slowdown in the progress of poverty reduction in the past 10 years was partially attributable to China's growth pattern driven by heavy investment in capital-intensive industries, and real estate development in urban sectors, while wages of rural and migrant workers have been growing at a much slower pace (Cai et al. 2009). The rising inequality in education and health outcomes in recent years in China, a subject addressed in Chap. 5, has also limited the ability of poor people to take advantage of expanding high-skilled job opportunities with much higher wages, which reinforces income inequality. Rising income inequality and widening social disparities can significantly slow future progress in reducing poverty, which is still one of China's major social issues in rural areas.

References

Biller D (2006) Sustainable development on the urban fringe. World Bank, Mimeo

Brautigam D (2011) The dragon's gift: the real story of China in Africa. Oxford University Press, Oxford

Cai Fang, Du Yang, Wang Meiyan (2009) Migration and labor mobility in China. UNDP Human Development report research paper

Chen S, Ravallion M (2007) China's (uneven) progress against poverty. J Develop Econ 82(1):1–42, http://academic.research.microsoft.com/Journal/4847/j-develop-econ-journal-of-development-economics

China National Bureau Statistics (2011) Poverty monitoring report of rural China 2010. China Statistics Press, Beijing

Dollar D (2007) Poverty, inequality and social disparities during China's economic reform. World Bank working paper

Fan S (2007) Linkages between government spending, growth and poverty in India and China. IFPRI, Washington, DC

Haughton J, Khandker S (2009) Handbook on poverty and inequality. The World Bank, Washington, DC

Hofman B, Wu J (2008) Explaining China's development and reforms. Commission on growth and development working paper no. 50

NBS (2010) Poverty monitoring and rural report. National Bureau of Statistics of China

Ravallion M (2009) A comparative perspective on poverty reduction in Brazil, China and India. World Bank policy research working paper, 5080

UNCADT (2011) World investment report 2011. United Nations Publication, New York/Geneva

World Bank (2009) Addressing China's water scarcity: recommendations for selected water resource management issues. The World Bank, Washington, DC

Chapter 3
Explaining China's Growth and Poverty Reduction Miracle

China's economic performance since the start of economic reform in 1978 is widely heralded as a growth miracle. Although many transitional and developing economies, such as Russia and India, have implemented similar economic reform policies over the past few decades, in the course of economic reform, many experienced economic volatility and political instability. These reforms brought only moderate economic growth to these countries. By contrast, China has managed to sustain a long period of growth at a record rate while also maintaining macroeconomic and social stability. This chapter has two focuses. First, it identifies key factors that underpin China's growth miracle. The second focus is to explain how China achieves the poverty reduction miracle.

3.1 How China Succeeded in Sustaining High Growth over Three Decades?

China's growth miracle has attracted global attention and spurred a proliferation of studies that have attempted to identify the factors underlying its unprecedented growth.[1] Five factors are broadly considered to be the key determinants of China's phenomenal growth performance.

[1] The key papers include Bosworth and Collins (2008), Chow and Li (2002), Chow (1993), Dekle and Vandenbroucke (2006), Fan and Zhang (2002), Hu and Khan (1997), Holz (2006a), IMF (2011), Kuijs and Wang (2006), Kwan (2006), Riedel et al. (2007), Keefer (2007), Lin et al. (2003), Lin and Liu (2000), Naughton (2006), El-Erian and Spence (2008), Knight et al. (2011), and Wang and Yao (2003).

X. Wang et al., *The Quality of Growth and Poverty Reduction in China*,
International Research on Poverty Reduction, DOI 10.1007/978-3-642-36346-7_3,

3.1.1 Economic Reform Policies

China's economic reform policies have been the key impetus behind the country's sustained growth. Over a span of 30 years, China's highly distorted and inefficient centrally planned economy was gradually transformed into an economic system that depends, to a great extent, on market forces to allocate resources, enforces private property rights, and operates within a set of relatively developed regulatory institutions.

The reform process started in the early 1980s in the agricultural sector through the introduction of household responsibility system and endorsement of TVEs, replacing the rural collective system. The decision of the 14th Party Congress in 1993 to establish a "socialist market economy" paved the way for the next stage of reforms in state-owned enterprises (SOEs) and the financial sector. The reform of SOEs involved devolution of management and control from the central government to managers of local enterprises and privatization of the majority of SOEs through the transfer of ownership of state assets. In the early 1990s, many SOEs were listed on the Shenzhen and Shanghai stock exchange. As SOE reform deepens, the private sector has become an increasingly dominant force in contributing to industrial output, with the private sector share of total industrial output rising from 6 % in 1998 to about 52 % in 2009 (China National Bureau Statistics 2010).

Another important structural reform involved fiscal and administrative decentralization from the central government to local tiers of institutions. Decentralization also created competition among local governments and improved efficiency through better decision-making based on local conditions and better information flows. These reforms unleashed enormous creativity and incentives of individuals, firms, and local governments that strived to maximize economic returns, by seeking out opportunities, both domestically and globally.

3.1.2 Government Commitment and the Chinese-Style Reform

History shows that growth entails much more than just economics. It requires the leadership of governments that are committed, credible, and capable. China's reform experience is a case in point. The Chinese government has evidently demonstrated its strong commitment and leadership to transform China from one of the poorest countries in the world to a prosperous middle-income nation by implementing a wide range of long-term economic reform programs, despite the challenges and political risks associated with these reforms.

China's approach to pursuing these reforms is unique. Chinese policymakers understood the enormous uncertainties brought about by economic reforms on such a scale. Following the principle developed by Deng Xiaoping "to cross the river by feeling for the stones," the Chinese government adopted a gradual, experimental, and pragmatic approach to reform, scaling up successful reforms over time and across regions based on an idea of learning by doing (Hofman and Wu 2008).

3.1.3 Strong Emphasis on Public Investment in Social Services and Rural Development

The third factor lies in China's long-term commitment to public investment in infrastructure, education and health, and basic environmental services both before and during the period of economic reforms. Although the centrally planned system had severely distorted resource allocation and hindered economic growth, progressive policies in promoting public investment in health, education, and access to safe water and sanitation services had laid the foundation for China's economic success once distortions and constraints were removed through economic reform (Sen 2009; Bardhan 2009).

Public investment policies prior to China's economic reform focused on expanding the population's access to basic health and education services in both urban and rural areas. Promoting gender equality was one of the key policy pillars. In the early 1980s, per capita income in China was much lower than India, Brazil, and Indonesia, even lower than Tanzania, but the social indicators, measured by child mortality, life expectancy, and adult female literacy rate, were far superior to these countries (see Table 3.1).

China's sustained growth in agricultural productivity since the early 1980s is largely attributed to its early investment in rural infrastructure (Table 3.1). Public investment in rural infrastructure, including electricity access, rural roads, and irrigation, laid the groundwork for the takeoff of rapid productivity growth in rural areas in the early 1980s when farmers were released from the constraints of collective farming institutions.

Essentially, prior to the transition to a market economy, China had built a literate and healthy labor force and developed an infrastructure base thanks to strong government-led investment in social services. When a conducive business climate was created by economic reform, the majority of the Chinese population had the capabilities to participate fully in the expanded economic opportunities brought by the reform policies, raising national income at a rapid pace.

3.1.4 Integration into the Global Economy

China's economic growth was further strengthened by its integration into the rest of the world. Indeed, the growth experience from 13 countries since the early 1970s,[2] all of which experienced an annual growth of 7 % or more over 25 years, highlights the importance of integration into the global economy for sustaining growth. Before 1950, sustained growth at a level of about 7 % was not conceivable. It was feasible only because the world economy became more open and integrated since the early 1970s (the Growth Commission and Development report 2008). The global economy

[2] These include Botswana, Brazil, China, Hong Kong, Indonesia, Japan, the Republic of Korea, Malaysia, Malta, Oman, Singapore, Taiwan, and Thailand (see The Growth Report 2008).

Table 3.1 Public investment: cross-country comparison

	Per capita income			Adult female	Improved water source	Agricultural irrigated land
	Constant US$	Child mortality	Life expectancy	literacy rate	% of population with access, 1989	% share in arable land, 1979–1981
China	194	62	67	1 (1981)	67	46.6
India	238	143	56	26	72	23.57
Brazil	3,303	87	63	73 (1979)	88	3.54
Russia	2,693 (1988)	33	67	96.8 (1988)	93	3.7 (1999–2001)
Indonesia	412	118	58	57.7 (1979)	71	23.38
Tanzania	292 (1987)	165	51	48.1 (1987)	55	4.02

Source: The World Bank database

offers China a nearly unlimited market for its export of goods and services while allowing it to improve efficiency and productivity by exploring its comparative advantage in low-cost labor and economies of scale. China's exports increased by more than eightfold from 1980 to 2010, overtaking Japan as the world's second largest exporter, just behind the United States.

The integration into the world economy also provides China with the opportunity to import technology and ideas, the know-how, and modern management skills that are embodied in foreign direct investment and joint ventures. By opening up its economy through trade and FDI, growth in the export sector also played a key role in stimulating technology upgrading.

Another important channel of knowledge transfer is through the exchange of people. Along with openness of trade and foreign investment, Chinese policymakers paid special attention to foreign education through exchange. The Chinese government invited a stream of foreign experts to help them learn about the functioning and features of a market economic system while at the same time sending many waves of Chinese students and government officials to be trained in US and European universities. Many prominent Chinese reformers were selected from the pool of Western-trained technocrats to be placed in key positions in China's economic reform policy think tanks, playing an important role in reshaping China's reform policymaking.

3.1.5 Industrial Upgrading and Technological Innovation

China's growth is largely driven by the process of learning and upgrading that results from the adoption of new technology embodied in FDI and massive capital investment. Schumpeter (1942) described this process as the process of "creative destruction."[3] China's rural TVEs have gone through the most dramatic transformation. In the early 1980s, they were based primarily on processing primary agricultural products, forestry, animal husbandry, and fisheries. Their operations gradually upgraded to produce goods of more technical content, such as textiles and apparel, electronics, chemicals, machinery metallurgy, modern food processing, and building materials, which now meet international quality standards.[4]

[3] Schumpeter (1942, p.83, his emphasis): "The fundamental impulse that sets and keeps the capitalist engine in motion comes from the new consumers' goods, the new methods of production or transportation, the new markets,...This process incessantly revolutionizes the economic structure from within, incessantly destroying the old one, incessantly creating a new one. This process of Creative Destruction is the essential fact about capitalism." Aghion and Howitt (1992) developed the endogenous growth models of creative destruction.

[4] Most of China's surge in exports has taken the form of processing manufactures operated by multinational companies taking advantage of low-cost Chinese labors. Using the combination of firm-level production data with product-level trade data, Fu (2011) shows that processing FDI has generated positive information spillover effects, such as market intelligence and marketing techniques on the export performance of indigenous firms, although the technological spillovers are found to hinder the performance of indigenous firms.

China has not only become the biggest exporter in the world, but its export structure had transformed dramatically since the early 1990s. There has been a sharp decline in the share of agriculture and low-skilled manufacturing products, such as textiles and apparel, while the share of hard manufacturers, such as consumer electronics, appliances, and computers, increased substantially.[5] The share of high-technology export in manufacturing increased from 6 % in 1992 to 31 % in 2009, as a result of rapid production upgrading in the industrial sector. The average productivity in manufacturing was only 5.6 % of that in the United States in 1995, but in less than a decade, it increased to 15.8 % by 2004, and coastal provinces have closed the technological gap with the international frontier.

China is now embarking on a new stage of production upgrading. Faced with increased resource constraints and the risk of global warming caused by carbon emissions, the Chinese government has committed to transforming China into a low-carbon and green economy. The development of strategic emerging industries (SEIs) is the key focus of the 12th Five-Year Plan, which includes biotechnology, new energy, high-end equipment manufacturing, energy generation and environmental protection, clean energy vehicles, new materials, and new generation information technology (IT). China has shifted investment toward clean technology. In 2009, China became the largest investor in clean energy technology—China's investment of $34.6 billion accounted for about 21 % of global total investment in clean energy.

China has also become the world's leading renewable energy producer, overtaking the United States in 2009 to become the leading investor in renewable energy technologies. China surpassed countries such as Denmark, Germany, Spain, and the United States in 2009 to become the world's largest maker of wind turbines and solar panels. China is also seeking to drive the development of green-energy technology and become the largest producer of alternative fuel vehicles in the world.

3.2 What Have Been the Sources of Growth?

3.2.1 Source of Growth by Factor

Numerous empirical studies that attempt to identify the sources of growth in China have concluded that China's record growth rate over the past several decades was sustained largely through growth in productivity (footnote lists these studies). This is clearly illustrated by the comparison of the sources of growth between China, India, and East Asia[6] as shown in Table 3.2.

---

[5] Some argue that a large component of this export growth in machinery is attributed to the growth in processing trade, i.e., assembling duty-free intermediate inputs of high skill content from developed economies such as the United States and Japan using low-cost Chinese laborers (Dean et al. 2007; Amiti and Freund 2008).

[6] East Asia also includes Indonesia, South Korea, Malaysia, Philippines, Singapore, Taiwan, and Thailand.

Table 3.2 Sources of growth by factor: comparison on China, India, and East Asia, 1978–2004

		1978–2004	(a) 1978–1993	(b) 1993–2004
China	GDP per worker (annual growth rate %)	7.3	6.4	8.5
	Contribution from			
	(1) Growth in capital per worker	3.2	2.4	4.2
	(2) Growth in years of schooling	0.3	0.4	0.3
	(3) Growth in total factor productivity	3.6	3.5	3.9
India	GDP per worker (annual growth rate %)	3.3	2.4	4.6
	Contribution from			
	(1) Growth in capital per worker	1.3	0.9	1.8
	(2) Growth in years of schooling	0.4	0.3	0.4
	(3) Growth in total factor productivity	1.6	1.1	2.3
		1980–2003	1980–1993	1993–2003
East Asia	GDP per worker (annual growth rate %)	3.7	6.4	2.5
	Contribution from			
	(1) Growth in capital per worker	2.2	2.6	1.8
	(2) Growth in years of schooling	0.5	0.6	0.5
	(3) Growth in total factor productivity	0.9	1.4	0.3

Source: Bosworth and Collins (2008)

During the period of 1978–2004, China saw a significant increase in labor productivity, measured by output per worker, at the annual rate of 7.3 %, compared with 3.3 % in India and 3.7 % in East Asia.[7] The improvement in labor productivity was driven mainly by capital investment and improvement in efficiency of factor usage and technological progress conventionally measured by total factor productivity (TFP).[8] The estimates from several sources (Bosworth and Collins 2008) show that growth in capital investment and TFP accounts for about 44 and 49 % of labor productive growth during 1978–2004, respectively.

[7] Using the firm-level data, Li et al. show that the median Chinese firm is 156 % more productive than the median Indian firm.

[8] Growth accounting approach provides an analytical framework for attributing changes in a country's GDP into contributions from changes in its factor inputs—capital and labor, plus a residual, typically named total factor productivity (TFP). TFP is interpreted as a measure of efficiency gains from factor input usages due to technology upgrading and improvement in management and business climate in general. The Cobb-Douglas production function is widely used for estimating TFP: $Y=AK\alpha(LH)$ $1-\alpha$ where Y, A, K, and α are measures of output, total factor productivity, physical capital services, and capital's share of income, respectively. The capital share α is usually assumed equal to 0.4–0.5. L and H are labor input and educational attainment (e.g., average years of schooling of the labor force). The product of L and H is adjusted labor input taking account of improvements in the level of skills. The growth per worker $\Delta\ln(Y/L)$ can be decomposed into growth in capital per worker $\Delta\ln(K/L)$, education per worker $\Delta\ln(H)$, and a residual measure of the contribution of improvements in total factor productivity $\Delta\ln(A)$ as expressed as $\Delta\ln(Y/L)=\alpha\,[\Delta\ln(K/L)]+(1-\alpha)\,\Delta\ln H+\Delta\ln A$. In interpreting the results from growth accounting decomposition, cautions should be taken because TFP captures anything unmeasured in the production function, except capital and labor input, ranging from technical progress and the effects of other determinants of the efficiency of factor usage, such as government policy, political region, and weather shocks.

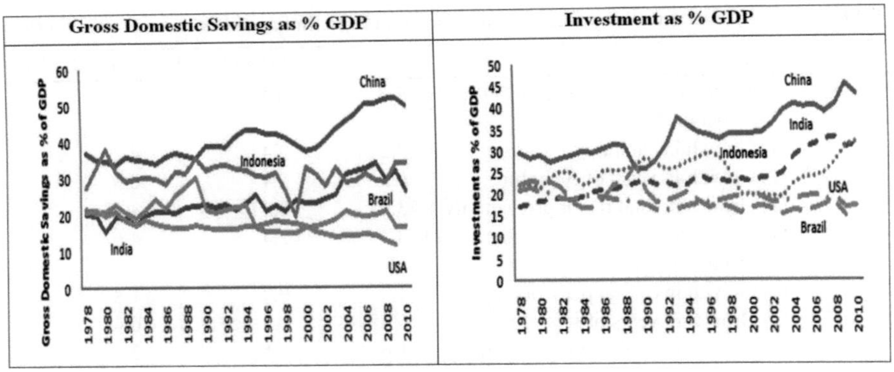

Fig. 3.1 Gross domestic savings and investment: China, India, Indonesia, and United States (*Source:* Constructed by authors based on World Bank data sources)

China's high savings rate made it possible to achieve a much faster capital accumulation rate than other countries (see Fig. 3.1). Physical capital per worker increased at an annual rate of 3.2 % during 1978–2004 in China, compared with 1.3 % in India and 2.2 % in East Asia as a whole (Table 3.2).

This growth in TFP sets China's growth performance apart from other fast-growing economies. Annual TFP growth in China increased from 1.1 % during 1953–1978 to 3.5 % during 1978–1993, again up to 3.9 % during 1993–2004 (Hu and Khan 1997). This is in sharp contrast with other countries: India experienced a TFP growth rate of 1.6 % during 1978–2004; East Asia, 0.9 % during 1980–2003; and the United States, 0.4 % during 1960–1969. While TFP growth accounts for nearly half of the increase in output per worker in China from 1978, for Asia as a whole during the same period, it only accounts for a quarter.

The Chinese economy has been in a virtuous circle with sustaining feedback effects: high investment produced rapid economic growth, and rapid growth in turn boosted expectations which then encouraged high investment. The positive interaction between investment and efficiency gained from both technological progress and resource reallocation is in line with what the endogenous growth theory predicts (Knight and Ding 2010). In short, China's fast and sustained economic growth is largely driven by improved efficiency usage of factor production and technological progress as reflected in the increase of labor productivity and total factor productivity during 1978–2000.

3.2.2 *Source of Growth by Sector*

China has undergone a significant change in the sectoral composition of the economy—transforming from an agriculture-based economy to an economy dominated by

Table 3.3 Sources of growth by sector: 1978–2004

	Total growth	Agriculture	Industry	Services	Reallocation
1978–1993					
Sectoral contribution to growth (%)	6.4	1.2	2.4	1.1	1.7
Output/per worker (annual growth rate %)	6.4	4.3	4.8	4.7	
1993–2004					
Sectoral contribution to growth (%)	8.5	0.7	5	1.7	1.2
Output/per worker (annual growth rate %)	8.5	4.3	9.8	5.1	

Source: Bosworth and Collins (2008)

industrial and services sectors. China's rapid increase in overall labor productivity is illustrated by the sectoral decomposition of growth accounting.

During the early period of reform, agriculture, industry, and services sectors were all growing at a high but comparable pace, ranging from 4.3 % for agriculture, 4.7 % for services, and 4.8 % for the industrial sector (see Table 3.3). As structural transformation accelerated, the industrial and services sectors overtook the agricultural sector during 1978–2004, with labor productivity growth in industry and services reaching 9.8 % and 5.1 %, respectively, compared with that of 4.3 % in the agricultural sector. These two sectors contributed about 59 and 20 % of total growth during 1993–2004, while the agricultural sector accounted for only 8 % (Bosworth and Collins 2008).

Within three decades, China completed the structural transformation from an agriculture-based economy to one dominated by the industrial sector, a process that took nearly two centuries to complete in Europe. More importantly, the declining importance of agriculture in the economy (in terms of labor force) is accompanied by sustained productivity growth in the agricultural sector, with an annual average growth of agricultural labor productivity of 4.8 % from 1991 to 2000, of 5.9 % from 2001 to 2005, and of 7.2 % from 2006 to 2009.

The productivity growth in the industrial sector further sustains China's overall growth. Firm-level evidence also confirms China's improved productivity in the industrial sector. The study based on firm-level data by Li et al. shows that TFP of Chinese firms is much higher than that of Indian firms. This productivity gap is attributed to the advantages the Chinese firms have over their Indian counterparts, including access to more skilled laborers employed in Chinese firms; higher returns to skills; better local infrastructure, in particular the reliability of power supply that is most critical for firms;[9] and greater labor market flexibility.

[9]The average proportion of annual sale lost due to power outages for Chinese firms is 2 % compared with 9 % for Indian firms based on the firm-level data (Li et al.).

The total productivity growth was also reinforced by the reallocation of resources between sectors. The shift of resources from a low-productivity agricultural sector to industry and services sectors was responsible for a large part of the efficiency gain in the economy. Based on estimates from several studies (Bosworth and Collins 2008), the reallocation effect explained about 25 % of total labor productivity growth in the reform period of 1978–1993 and for about 15 % in the following period from 1993 to 2004 (see Table 3.3). The Chinese experience is consistent with what was observed in a range of countries, i.e., the importance of the reallocation effect on growth, in addition to growth from individual sectors, in explaining the overall growth rate.

In conclusion, China's growth, in particular, in the 1980s and 1990s, could be attributable to a wide range of domestic factors that underpinned productivity growth. These include carefully designed economic reform policies based on China's specific circumstances, an experimental and pragmatic approach to implementing these polices, the strong leadership of the government that is credible and committed, and a long tradition of public investment focusing on human capital, basic environmental services (safe water and sanitation), and rural development. The integration into the global economy, through FDI and expansion of export sectors, has provided a further catalyst to China's economic growth, with the global economy serving both as a massive market for China's exports and as a source of knowledge, including technology, management skills, ideas, and information that underpin the production upgrading.

The important role of government in human capital development and rural investment laid the foundation for the rapid productivity growth in the agricultural sector when rural institutional reforms were implemented, which spurred China's economic transformation from an agricultural economy to one dominated by industrial and services sectors within a period of less than three decades.

While there are few empirical studies on the sources of growth during the 2000s, many indicators suggest that the sectoral productivity growth and efficiency gain from resource reallocation between sectors became less important sources in driving China's overall growth during this period. Some evidence from the firm-level study (Eberhardt et al. 2011) confirms such conclusions. The production upgrading of many Chinese companies that was made possible through FDI and joint ventures was mainly through assembling and processing operations, rather than technological progress and innovation. The majority of Chinese companies did not catch up with their counterparts in the developed economies in technology development and innovation, despite their rapid expansion of production driven by a large domestic market and export. A pertinent question in the coming decade remains as to how China can sustain its growth when overreliance on capital accumulation and export becomes a binding constraint, while the efficiency gain from resource allocation between sectors and the comparative advantage of low-cost labor diminish.

3.3 How China Achieve the Poverty Reduction Miracle?

3.3.1 The Theoretical Foundation

3.3.1.1 The Conception of Poverty

With human society's deeper understanding of poverty, various disciplines have defined and analyzed poverty from different perspectives. Economists define and measure poverty from an economic perspective, and sociologists analyze poverty from the perspective of social exclusion and social inclusion, while philosophers and political scientists explore poverty from the perspective of rights. This chapter first reviews the relevant literature in relation to three aspects, namely, the economic dimensions, capability approach, and social exclusion, and then builds its theoretical framework for triangular poverty reduction.

Economic Dimensions

"Poverty" is usually defined as a state of privation, or a lack of the usual or socially acceptable amount of money or material possessions (*Encyclopedia Britannica*). In his book *Poverty: A Study of Town Life*, published in 1901, Benjamin Seebohm Rowntree estimates the poverty line of the city of York in the United Kingdom based on the monetary budget for a "shopping basket" to "meet the minimum physical needs." For a family of six people, the minimum weekly food budget is 15 shillings; plus shelter, clothing, fuel, and other items, the poverty line for a family of six is 26 shillings a week. At the time, the incidence of poverty in York was 10 % or so (Kanbur and Squire 1999, p. 3). This is the earliest definition of poverty using monetary quantification based on two parts: food and nonfood. Later, this method was applied to most countries and regions in the world to varying extents.

A typical example of poverty definition and measurement in accordance with the amount of money comes from the World Bank. The World Bank defines and measures poverty in accordance with the cost of basic needs. Basic needs include two parts: first, access to a certain amount of food for adequate nutrition, mostly based on calorie intake of 2,100 cal per person per day, and second, clothing, housing, and other nonfood basic needs (World Bank 2009a, b). In fact, this shows the legacy of Rowntree's 1901 approach. Ravallion collected the consumption data for 86 countries (including both developed and developing countries) in the period from 1980 to 1990 and found that the lowest per capita consumption was US$ 22/month (1985 PPP dollars), very close to India's poverty line of US$ 23/month at that time. The absolute poverty line of eight low-income countries (Indonesia, Bangladesh, Nepal, Kenya, Tanzania, Morocco, the Philippines, and Pakistan), however, was US$ 31 per day, which was a more typical absolute poverty line. This is the source of the absolute poverty line of US$ 1 a day. In 2008, Ravallion, Chen, and Sangraula revised the poverty line of "US$ 1/day." They selected 75 developing countries (including transition countries) for a survey and found the average poverty line of 15 poorest countries was US$ 37.98/month (US$ 1.25/day) and the median was US$ 38.51/month. This is the source of the widely applied poverty line of US$ 1.25 a day in the World Bank's *World Development Report* and the UN's Millennium Development Goals. This definition of poverty from an economic perspective has long occupied the central position of studies on poverty reduction. The main policy instrument for poverty reduction is of course the increase of income or issuing of income support policy.

Capability Approach

According to the traditional definition, poverty is a phenomenon of deprivation of well-being, which is usually measured in terms of an amount of money to meet certain "basic needs." It is undeniable that inadequate income is a very strong condition inducing poverty, and revenues can be used to meet the "basic needs" so as to improve well-being or shake off poverty. In fact, income is only a tool to achieve a certain level of well-being, while improved quality of life is the real purpose. It is thus clear that too much attention to income poverty tends to make public policy deviate from the true purpose of improving the quality of life. We should, therefore, analyze poverty from a new perspective. Amartya Sen's book *Development as Freedom* contains an in-depth discussion "looking at poverty from the perspective of capability," which is a revolutionary leap in the history of human understanding of poverty.

Sen's capability approach or concept of capability poverty is influenced by Adam Smith. According to Smith, a person's capability to appear in public places without shame is the basic need. The lack of such basic need is poverty. To present at a meeting, according to Smith, a person should have a linen shirt. Based on Smith's opinion, Sen believes that the ability to appear in public places without shame is an absolute capability, while the need for a linen shirt to build such a capacity is a kind of relative need for social interaction. Sen points out that we have good reasons to believe poverty is a kind of deprivation of basic capabilities rather than low income. Deprivation of basic capabilities can take the form of premature mortality, significant malnutrition (especially for children), sustained incidence of illness, widespread illiteracy, and other deficiencies (Sen 1999, p. 20).

Sen's contribution is that he further extended the logic of the definition of poverty, i.e., "poverty – wellbeing's being deprived – basic needs – ability." Sen believes that there are more policy implications if poverty is understood from the perspective of capability deprivation. First, poverty can be easily identified by the deprivation of ability. Sen's approach is more concerned about the substance of being deprived, while income is merely a means or instrument to identify poverty. Second, income is not the only instrument to build ability, and there are other factors that affect capacity deprivation. Third, the instrumental relations between low income and low ability are variable in different communities, different families, and different individuals. For example, the relationship between income and ability is affected by a person's age (elderly people and children have special needs), gender and social role (e.g., mother's specific responsibilities or common family obligations), geographic location (prone to floods or droughts, urban insecurity, or violence), epidemic breeding environment, and some other factors that individuals cannot or can hardly control (Sen 1999, pp. 87–88). This indicates that income's transformation into capability is affected by many factors.

The capability approach's analysis of the causes of poverty extends to rights. Sen carried out in-depth analysis of the relationship between famine and rights and found that the great famines in many countries were not caused by inadequate food, but occurred because the food could not be allocated to people in need. Therefore, Sen believes that the cause of famine is unequal rights. Famine occurs in a country as some of its people have too much to eat, while the others have to endure hunger. The unequal rights and unequal distribution are the causes of starvation. Therefore, in order to eliminate hunger, we must first eliminate the inequality.

Sen believes that we must empower the poor in many aspects, including production, exchange, and liquidity, in order to make them live a decent life. Land is the fundamental guarantee for a family to produce enough food and eliminate hunger, but the poor in many countries do not have the right to produce on land. Exchange is a condition for laborers to obtain other commodities and services with their land outputs to improve the quality of their lives. In some countries and regions, however, free exchange of commodities and services is forbidden, resulting in family poverty. Migration ensures that people can find development opportunities in migration. According to UNDP's research, the domestic population mobility of various countries and international migration all show that more development opportunities can be found in the process of migration and that population mobility helps eliminate poverty.

Social Exclusion

Sociologists divide poverty into deprivation and social exclusion based on the analysis of the social disadvantages of individuals or families. The concept of deprivation is mainly used to identify the poor and help set the poverty line, such as measuring income poverty. Accordingly, social exclusion is mainly used to identify people who have been excluded from the welfare system and those who are unable to participate in social and economic activities. Social exclusion provides a broader perspective for the analysis of poverty and it is more closely linked with institutional structure.

The concept of deprivation focuses on being deprived due to the lack of resources, which results in poverty. It helps identify who is poor and how much income they need to eliminate their state of being deprived. Defining poverty based on this idea consists of three steps: first, determine which goods and services are required, i.e., the basic needs discussed earlier; second, make clear who lacks these goods and services; and third, distinguish between those who cannot afford necessary goods and services and who have the ability to pay but do not want to. Those who cannot afford necessary goods and services are finally identified as poverty-stricken people.

Social exclusion is the process of some individuals being marginalized due to their inability to completely integrate into society because of poverty, a lack of basic competencies and lifelong learning opportunities, or discrimination. This process leads to these individuals rarely getting jobs, incomes, or opportunities for education and training. As a result, they cannot participate in social and community networks and activities. "Social exclusion" is defined by UNDP as the status of basic civil and social rights not being recognized (such as the access to adequate health care, education, and other nonphysical forms of welfare) and the lack of necessary political and legal system channels to realize these rights in these regions.

Most scholars believe some systems are the causes of the phenomenon of social exclusion, including: (1) democratic and legal systems, (2) the labor market system, (3) the social welfare system, and (4) family and community systems. The study of social exclusion from the system perspective, therefore, aims at eliminating social exclusion from a country or a region's top-level design of political, economic, cultural, and social systems.

The concept of poverty as deprivation makes people pay more attention to the phenomenon itself, while the concept of social exclusion makes people more concerned about the nature or cause of the phenomenon. In this sense, the proposal and widespread application of the concept of social exclusion is a theoretical refinement of the understanding of poverty. Poverty and deprivation make people believe poverty is linked to insufficient economic resources. Social exclusion, however, makes people think about political, economic, cultural, and social systems (Wang Xiaolin 2012).

3.3.1.2 The Framework of Triangular Poverty Reduction

The above literature review of poverty definitions shows that the definition of poverty from an economic perspective emphasizes the importance of growth, which is also the core content of growth theory study in development economics. The definition of poverty from a capability perspective emphasizes the importance of public services and empowerment. The analysis of poverty from the perspective of social exclusion, however, stresses the significance of social policy and social systems in poverty reduction. But these theories cannot completely explain China's poverty reduction miracle. Scholars of different disciplines may explain development from different perspectives, but development itself cannot be segmented because of the division of disciplines.

China's experience is unique. China's policy has a very strong oriental cultural context, usually manifested by the national leaders' speeches and reports, five-year plans, and the relevant institutions and policies. This chapter, therefore, summarizes the key elements of China's development strategies since the central government

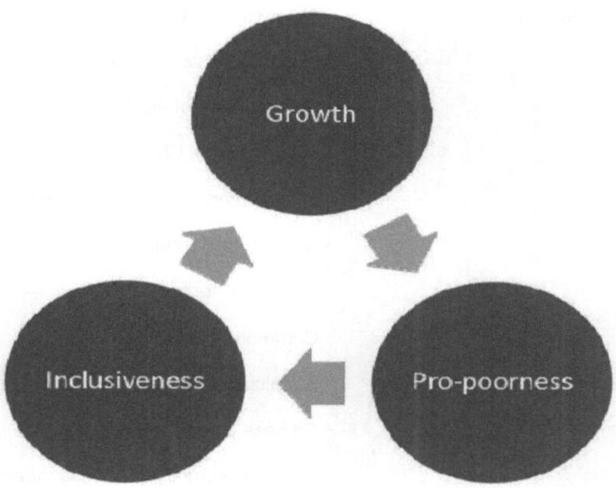

Fig. 3.2 Theoretical framework for triangular poverty reduction

under the leadership of Deng Xiaoping to establish a theoretical framework, in a Chinese context. The chapter then attempts to explain this framework using some of the existing Western concepts of economics, human development, social policy, political science, etc., aiming at establishing the analytical framework in a Western context.

The core idea of China's development theory since 1978 can be briefly summarized as follows using China's political slogans: *liberate the productive forces; develop the productive forces; people-oriented, comprehensive, coordinated, and sustainable development; and the Chinese dream.*

These political slogans for development actually include the economic, political, sociological, and philosophical ideas for managing state affairs, trying to guide China to grow into a "prosperous" nation and eradicate poverty. Based on China's development and poverty reduction over the past three decades, this chapter uses the term "theoretical framework for growth-promoting—inclusive—pro-poor triangle of poverty reduction" (Fig. 3.2). Figure 3.3 compares the Chinese and Western contexts of triangular poverty reduction.

Growth is the basis for development. The phenomenon of growth without development often occurs in the world. That is to say, the quality of growth is rather poor, and most people cannot benefit from growth. The emergence of this situation creates the need for quality of growth and access to equal opportunity for participation in growth, leading to inclusive development and resulting in pro-poor growth.

As for how to promote a country's growth, development economists have a variety of theoretical explanations. When development economics became a branch of modern economics after World War II, structuralists believed economic structure is exogenously determined, emphasizing market failure and the role of government in changing the economic structure and promoting economic development, which was the mainstream idea at the time. As the policy of government-led upgrading of industrial structure proposed by structuralists was seen to fail in developing countries, after the 1970s, development economics

Dimension	Chinese Context	Western Context
Growth	Liberation of productive forces Development of productive forces Invigoration of China through the development of science and education Science and technology as primary productive forces	Empowerment Fairness Human capital investment Scientific and technological progress
Inclusiveness	Common prosperity Equalization of basic public services Chinese dream Equal opportunity to have wonderful lives	Equal opportunity Social inclusion
Pro-poorness	People-oriented nature Letting the people share the achievements of reform and opening up Development-oriented poverty reduction Social security	All people Pro-poorness Social security

Fig. 3.3 Chinese and Western contexts of the theoretical framework for triangular poverty reduction (*Source*: Created by the author)

turned to take the "Washington Consensus" as the mainstream idea, stressing government failure and the role of the market and ignoring structure and transition. Lin Yifu proposed the theoretical framework for new structural economics. He believed that endogenous economic structure is determined by the endowment structure and advocated the use of a new method adapted from classical economics for study of economic structure and its changes, as well as the role of governments and markets, to compensate for the current shortcomings of development economics (Lin 2012).

This chapter focuses on explaining why China's high growth over the past three decades led to large-scale poverty reduction. Whether for individuals, enterprises, or countries, to achieve growth, we must have equal and adequate rights to use factors of production. The theoretical framework in this chapter, therefore, includes three core contents. First, make sure there is a certain rate of growth. Growth will benefit the poor through a "trickle-down effect," thus contributing to poverty reduction. Second, equal access to opportunities for various entities involved in economic growth should be provided. Growth cannot exclude some groups, especially the vulnerable, for institutional or policy reasons. Third, the government should issue income distribution policy and social security policy to ensure the growth will benefit the poor. Otherwise, along with the growth process, the social gap will continue to widen.

3.3.2 *From Growth to Poverty Reduction*

3.3.2.1 Liberate the Productive Forces

There are two ways to reduce poverty: economic growth and income distribution. From 1978 to 2000, the fundamental driving force of poverty reduction was high growth. Deng Xiaoping put forward that China's fundamental method of eradicating poverty lies in "liberating the productive forces" and the "developing productive forces."

The development theory that is most closely related to "liberating the productive forces" is Amartya Sen's rights and poverty theory, i.e., empowering the poor. Sen believes that the root cause of poverty is the deprivation of basic practical ability, i.e., the deprivation of rights. Therefore, elimination of poverty means not only an increase in the income of the poor but also the elimination of root causes of poverty, i.e., improving the basic practical ability of poverty-stricken people and giving the poor equal rights to development. Sen stressed that hunger is a result of the fact that some people are not provided enough food and is not caused by inadequate food in the world. A statement about the food supply is about a commodity (or a group of commodities) itself, but a statement on hunger is about the relationship between a person and the commodity (or a group of commodities), i.e., the relation between people and goods. Hunger is basically human's food ownership relation. The ownership relation is one of the rights relations. Therefore, we should analyze hunger and poverty as a relationship of rights.

The basic rights to human equality in development and freedom from hunger can be summarized as economic rights and political rights. Sen summarized the typical rights relations in the market economy of private ownership as follows: (1) Production-based rights: products made with one's own resources or the resources a person hired on a voluntary basis. (2) Trade-based rights: a person is entitled to own something he/she got through voluntary exchange (in multilateral trade, there is a collection of voluntary participants). (3) Labor rights: a person has the right to have his/her own ability to work and thus has the trade-based right related to his/her work ability as well as production-based rights. (4) Inherited and transferred rights: a person has the right to own whatever others give him/her on a voluntary basis, but the ownership of these goods should be legal, and such gifts may be ineffective until the granter dies. Based on this framework, Sen believes that the root cause of poverty is deprivation of rights. Accordingly, empowerment is the key to poverty reduction.

China has given farmers the most extensive rights through institutional reform. The empowerment process has been gradually reflected in the land reform, agricultural price reform, reform of labor mobility, development of township enterprises by farmers, etc.

Land Reform: Giving Farmers Production-Based Rights and Labor Rights. China has a big population and a small land area. China's per capita arable land area is less than 0.1 ha. On such a limited arable land area, to solve the poverty problem and let all Chinese people have enough to eat, we must first address the rights relation between humans and land and then solve relevant technical problems. On this basis, the Chinese governments in various dynasties all took land reform as an important institutional arrangement to stabilize the overall situation of China.

In 1978, through the household land contract system reform, China once again gave all farmers equal arable land resources. On their contracted land, farmers own production-based rights and their labor rights. As for the system, through the household contract responsibility system, China gave farmers the right to produce on land freely, effectively encouraging farmers to conduct production with the best mode. According to Lin Yi Fu's study (1992), from 1978 to 1984, the household contract responsibility system contributed 42.2–46.9 % to the agricultural growth. Through the household contract responsibility system, each peasant household acquired land. As long as it has labor ability, the household can produce a certain amount of food to cope with hunger. At this stage, there was a decline of 125 million in the number of poverty-stricken people in China.

Agricultural Price Reform: Giving Farmers Trade-Based Rights. The household contract system stimulated the enthusiasm of farmers for production. Farmers had increasing surplus agricultural products. In addition to their own consumption, they needed to exchange products. To this end, the Chinese government launched a progressive reform to gradually liberalize agricultural prices. From 1979 to 1984, although the national acquisition policy in the planned economy period remained, the government began to significantly raise the procurement prices of agricultural products and by-products including grain, oil plants, sugar, etc. From 1984 to 1991, the dual pricing system reform led to some products being purchased by the government and some being priced by the market. In 1992, China started the comprehensive construction of a market pricing-based agricultural price system. In 2001, China joined the World Trade Organization and entered the global agricultural market. After that, it further established an agricultural support price system and implemented the subsidy system for grain farmers. The liberalization of agricultural markets and prices not only gave farmers the right to free exchange of surplus products on the market but also ensured that the farmers could choose the best way to produce based on market information.

Population Movement: Giving Farmers the Right to Choices and Migrant Work in the City in Migration. Limited arable land and a big population led to the existence of a large number of surplus laborers in rural China. In 1984, the Chinese government began to encourage farmers to work in township enterprises and later gradually encouraged them to work in the city or in the industrial sector. Meanwhile, it set up a large number of labor transfer markets and launched many labor transfer training projects to promote population migration and mobility. Although many scholars criticized population "migration and mobility," there is no doubt that migration and mobility can bring more development opportunities. Problems arising from migration and mobility are all problems in development.

In 1978, China liberalized restrictions on labor mobility, allowing land subcontracting and allowing farmers to work or do business in the city. From 1979 to 1985, 45.77 million rural laborers transferred from the agricultural industry to nonfarming sectors, and hundreds of thousands of farmers stayed in the city doing business throughout the year as a floating population. The number of temporary migrant workers reached 6 million per year (Zhou 2002). In 2012, there were a total of 262.61 million migrant workers in China, of whom 163.36 million worked in the city for at least 6 months and 99.25 million worked within local towns for at least 6 months. Wage income accounted for more than 40 % of farmers' net income. Population flow brought opportunities for a substantial increase in cash income of farmers.

China encourages the establishment of systems for large-scale population movement and gives farmers the right to exchange their labor and the right to work in the city and nonfarming sectors, increasing nonfarming income and effectively reducing rural poverty.

Entrepreneurship: Giving Farmers the Right to Entrepreneurship and Wealth Inheritances. Land empowerment for farmers not only stimulated the growth of agricultural production but also brought a surplus workforce. By allowing free movement of labor and giving farmers the right to free exchange of labor, farmers' income was increased and poverty effectively reduced. With the increase of farmers' income, we need to further expand production. Therefore, the Chinese government encourages farmers to start their own businesses and launch township enterprises, allows the development of the private economy, and has established the economic system to protect private property and allow inheritance of property. A constitutional amendment protects private property and gives people the right to inheritance of property. Since 1978, the number of migrant workers in township enterprises has been increasing.

Adjustments of the above rights relationship are the innovations of China's economic system to liberate the productive forces. These economic system innovations reallocated rights and, through empowering farmers, promoted economic growth and poverty reduction, laying an institutional basis for China's large-scale poverty reduction.

3.3.2.2 Develop the Productive Forces

According to Sen, "hunger is not only dependent on food supply, but also on the distribution of food." Distribution is the adjustment of rights relations. Through the liberation of productive forces, China successfully gave farmers the most basic rights system for poverty reduction. Supply, however, lays particular emphasis on the technical level and is a technical issue. China mainly develops productive forces through large-scale technological advances in agricultural development. In other words, adjustment-based institutional arrangements relating to rights relations are designed to give equal rights to each farmer. To improve production efficiency, however, we cannot just depend on the adjustment of rights relations, but need large-scale technological progress. Deng Xiaoping put forward in 1988 that science and technology are primary productive forces and we should develop the productive forces through scientific and technological progress (Deng Xiaoping 1994).

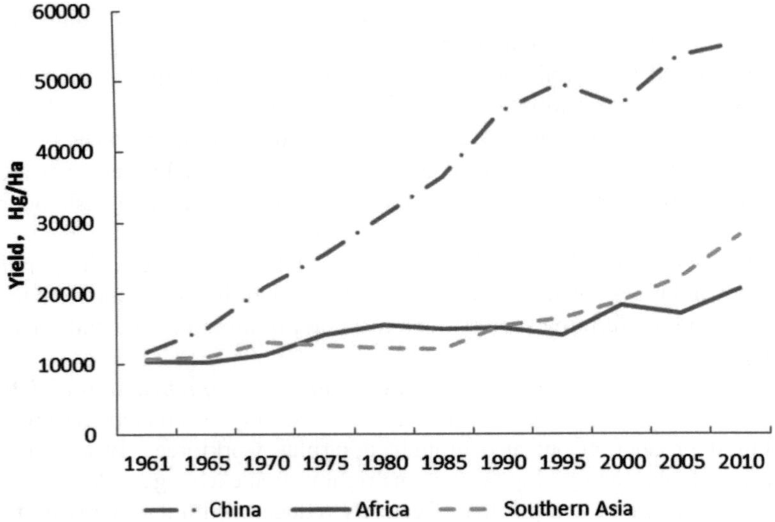

Fig. 3.4 Comparison of maize yield from 1961 to 2009 (*Source*: FAOSTAT)

According to Yujiro Hayami and Ruttan's "Induced Technique - Institutional Innovation Model", in a market economy, affected and induced by changes in factor prices, farmers will be committed to pursuing techniques that can replace increasingly scarce factors of production. In the process of development of the agricultural economy, resource endowments' decisive influence on technology choice and the significance of technological change in agricultural development also lie in the demand and supply of institutional change and the relationship between technical innovation and institutional reform. In most economies, agricultural output growth is essential to the agricultural development process, and the nature of agricultural development is "to accelerate the growth of agricultural output and productivity in order to make it consistent with the growth of other components of a department of modernized economy." In order to achieve growth in agricultural productivity, a necessary condition is advancement in technology and institutional innovation. Technology development can promote relatively common (thus cheaper) elements in economies to replace relatively scarce (thus expensive) elements. Moreover, through in-depth development of scarce factors (such as land), technology can also change their scarcity to some extent. China's agricultural development process verified this theory. As the land element is scarce and per capita arable land is less than 0.1 ha, Chinese farmers have to seek technological advances in agriculture as an alternative to the relatively scarce land element. We can see from Fig. 3.4 that in 1961, there was little difference in maize yields between China and Africa or Southern Asia. After that, however, China's food technology progress was much faster than that in Africa and Southern Asia. The increase in grain yield was a result of technological progress and institutional change, not dependent on the land resource endowments.

Development of productive forces relies on scientific and technological progress, and the core of scientific and technological progress is human capital investment, mainly for education, health care, etc. China has made significant progress in education and health care. We do not talk about that here.

Agricultural technology itself has the nature of a public product, manifested in two ways: the market cannot allocate resources efficiently to provide public goods for a large number of customers beyond recognition, and new information or new knowledge generated from study has the external economic nature of noncompetitiveness or communalism in supply and use. The former means that everyone can have equal access to this product, while the latter means that it is impossible for private producers of agricultural technology products to generate all social benefits of direct product making and consumption through market pricing. It is impossible to reach the socially optimal supply level simply relying on markets and nonprofit organizations to provide agricultural technical services. In this process, we should make various institutional arrangements based on the characteristics of agricultural technology such as fundamentality and application, i.e., the size of externalities. Since reform and opening up, China's agricultural technology has gradually formed a network participated in by the government, research institutions, businesses, and farmers, all playing a positive role. Although this network is still imperfect, it has provided important technical support for China's agricultural economic development.

3.3.3 From Inclusiveness to Poverty Reduction

In this chapter, the inclusiveness connotes equal opportunity and pro-poorness is determined through fair results. As mentioned above, China has achieved sustained rapid economic growth through the liberation and development of productive forces, resulting in large-scale poverty reduction. In 2006, however, China's Gini coefficient reached the highest level in history. With the high growth, inequality has become increasingly prominent. The growing regional development disparities and widening development and wealth gap between urban and rural areas have excluded the poor from development. Especially since the 2008 global financial crisis, the Chinese economy has also been affected. In 2013, China's economic growth slowed down significantly. The poverty reduction through the "trickle-down effect" of economic growth faces great challenges. The emergence of unequal distribution of income along with economic growth also makes it difficult for growth to benefit the poor.

Table 3.4 analyzes the contribution of China's economic growth and income distribution to the incidence of poverty with an econometric model. The results show that from 1989 to 2009, China's poverty rate dropped from 56.64 to 11.39 %, with a decrease of 45.25 percentage points. Income growth, income distribution, and the interaction of growth and distribution, respectively, contributed −55.5 %, 33.03 %, and −22.78 % to poverty incidence.

The above analysis shows that the income distribution from 1989 to 2009 was not conducive to poverty reduction. To further analyze the impact of inequality on poverty reduction, Table 3.5 provides the impact of unfairness on the Foster-Greer-Thorbecke poverty reduction measurement, including the impact of the Gini coefficient on

Table 3.4 Contribution of growth and distribution to changes in the incidence of poverty

	Poverty rate					
	1989	2009	Change	Growth	Distribution	Interaction
Total	56.64	11.39	−45.25	−55.50	33.03	−22.78
Urban areas	67.89	6.64	−61.25	−67.16	28.53	−22.62
Rural areas	38.15	13.59	−24.56	−36.95	44.68	−32.29

Source: Wang (2012)

Table 3.5 Impact of inequality on poverty

	Poverty rate (P0)			Poverty gap index (P1)			Squared poverty gap index (P2)		
Year	Urban areas	Rural areas	Total	Urban areas	Rural areas	Total	Urban areas	Rural areas	Total
1989	0.04	1.68	0.43	1.06	2.89	1.56	1.97	2.80	2.36
1991	0.07	0.20	0.18	1.19	1.40	1.38	5.42	4.69	5.20
1993	0.46	0.48	0.55	1.87	1.69	1.87	2.86	2.81	3.03
1997	0.83	0.92	0.87	2.20	2.59	2.58	3.43	3.83	3.85
2000	1.10	1.23	1.40	3.00	3.19	3.44	4.43	4.51	4.77
2004	1.14	1.62	1.74	4.01	3.62	4.07	3.72	−0.26	0.30
2006	2.42	2.21	2.49	5.33	4.79	5.35	6.81	5.70	6.26
2009	4.24	5.01	5.25	6.58	5.72	6.07	5.69	2.54	2.66

Source: Wang (2012)

Table 3.6 Inequality (Gini) in per capita disposable income by urban and rural areas

Year	Total	Urban	Rural
1989	36.96	31.94	44.06
1991	41.80	35.06	44.53
1993	47.04	41.23	48.44
1997	45.82	41.98	47.12
2000	47.27	41.43	48.71
2004	49.82	43.13	51.55
2006	51.19	44.35	53.69
2009	48.92	40.92	51.96

poverty incidence (P0), on the poverty gap index (P1), and on the squared poverty gap index (P2). The policy implication of the above analysis is that from 1989 to 2009, with constant revenue growth, improved income distribution could have further reduced the incidence of poverty. This also indicates that in the coming period, income distribution should be an important policy for poverty reduction.

Table 3.6 shows that in 2009, each additional percentage point in the Gini coefficient resulted in an increase of 4.24 percentage points in the incidence of urban poverty and an increase of 5.01 percentage points in the incidence of rural poverty.

The deterioration of the income distribution situation undermined the poverty reduction effect of growth. In order to achieve sustained poverty reduction, the Chinese government put forward that we should "let the fruits of reform and opening up benefit the entire population" and "make everyone have access to opportunities for wonderful life." After these new political slogans were put forward, China issued a series of policies to promote inclusive development.

Within the values of China's current development policy, inclusive development policy is intended to "continue to safeguard social fairness and justice," i.e., to gradually establish the system for protection of social fairness and justice with equal opportunities and fairness of rights and rules, strive to create a fair social environment, and ensure equal right for people's participation and development.[10] Recently, Chinese President Xi Jinping put forward the development idea of the "Chinese dream" and further emphasized equality of opportunity. That is to say, all people should have equal opportunities to enjoy a wonderful life, realize their dreams, and grow together with their motherland and the era.

Zhuangju Zhong believes that to achieve inclusive growth, developing countries should take the following measures: first, increase investment in basic education, basic health care, and other basic social services to improve the basic abilities and capabilities of vulnerable groups; second, increase policy and system fairness, eliminate social injustice, and improve the market mechanism to create conditions for equal competition; and third, establish social risk prevention mechanisms to prevent and eradicate extreme poverty. Recalling China's public policies over the past decade, China is gradually introducing inclusive policies to promote social justice and eradicate poverty.

3.3.4 From Pro-poor Policies to Poverty Reduction

China's pro-poor development policies include special poverty alleviation policies represented by development-oriented poverty reduction and the minimum living security policy. Development-oriented poverty reduction targets the poor with the ability to work, aiming to lift them out of poverty through government and social support. The minimum living security system mainly provides cash support for people living below the absolute poverty line.

As a means of government regulation to compensate for market survival of the fittest and increase pro-poorness, China's development-oriented poverty reduction aims to promote pro-poor growth. That is, through special poverty alleviation and development, the aim is to incorporate the regions and people lagging behind in the market into the development policies and give poverty-stricken regions and people equal opportunities for development. Under the guidance of this theory, the Chinese government has developed a multidimensional, government-led special poverty alleviation and development system participated in by communities. The main contents of this system include the following:

First, set up a special leading group under the State Council to be responsible for the coordination of poverty reduction departments, namely, the State Council Leading Group of Poverty Alleviation and Development. The Vice-Premier of the

[10] Hu Jintao's report delivered at the 18th National Congress of the CPC on Nov. 8, 2012.

Table 3.7 Dynamic change in China's relative poverty (1989–2009)

	Poverty rate (P_0)			Poverty gap index (P_1)			Squared poverty gap index (P_2)		
Year	Urban	Rural	Total	Urban	Rural	Total	Urban	Rural	Total
1989	1.8	3.0	2.3	4.0	5.9	4.7	28.6	96.4	54.2
1991	7.7	13.0	11.3	5.2	9.1	7.8	5.8	13.8	11.2
1993	8.0	13.9	12.0	6.6	9.5	8.6	17.8	12.0	13.8
1997	11.3	14.9	13.7	6.8	10.8	9.5	7.1	17.0	13.9
2000	12.6	15.7	14.7	7.9	9.7	9.1	7.8	12.4	10.9
2004	13.6	17.9	16.5	9.2	14.0	12.4	9.9	28.8	22.4
2006	10.1	19.1	16.1	6.2	13.7	11.2	5.3	21.3	16.0
2009	6.6	13.6	11.4	4.1	10.7	8.6	5.7	104.2	73.0
1989–2009	4.8	10.6	9.1	0.2	4.8	3.9	−22.9	7.8	18.8

Source: Wang (2012)

State Council is the team leader, and the Leading Group is mainly responsible for coordinating more than 30 ministries in poverty alleviation and development. As poverty is a multidimensional phenomenon, China set up this deliberative institution to promote poverty reduction. Under the Leading Group, LGOP was set up to take charge of daily affairs. Similar agencies have been set up in various provinces, cities, and counties.

Second, since 2001, versions of "China's Rural Poverty Alleviation and Development Program" have been developed every decade. The program provides the targets, objectives, and tasks of the antipoverty work for the decade as well as the monitoring and evaluation methods and policies. The current "China's Rural Poverty Alleviation and Development Program (2011–2020)" is divided into three levels of action: identified *128 million* poverty-stricken farmers (2011) with annual per capita net income below 2,300 yuan (2010 constant prices) as the objects of poverty reduction; determined 592 poor counties in the country, for which the government will strive to promote economic and social development through fiscal transfer payments and special poverty alleviation and development; and identified 14 contiguous impoverished areas with special difficulty as the priority target of regional economic development, for which the government will develop special policies to promote balanced regional development.

Third, the government has set up a special budget to promote the implementation of the poverty reduction program and has established the "trinity" (special poverty alleviation, social poverty alleviation, and industry (sector) poverty alleviation) working mechanism, aiming to form a poverty reduction pattern jointly participated in by the government, market, and social organizations.

Through the implementation of inclusive and pro-poor policies, China's relative poverty and Gini coefficient both began to decline after 2006 (Table 3.6). Despite people's growing discontent with the widening income gap since the reform and opening up, the results in Table 3.7 show that a series of inclusive and pro-poor policies implemented in China since 2006 have now had a significant policy effect.

3.4 Summary

This section establishes a growth-promoting—inclusive—pro-poor triangular theoretical framework to explain how the high growth in China can bring large-scale poverty reduction. The core theory to promote growth is "liberating and developing the productive forces." The core of liberating the productive forces is to give everyone the right to participate in economic activities through fair competition. The core of the development of productive forces is scientific and technological progress and human capital investment. Thanks to the continuing system innovations and practices to promote inclusive and pro-poor growth, China has achieved sustainable poverty reduction.

However, the new challenges of climate change and persistent poverty clustered in extremely ecologically fragile areas of China present a strong case for promoting a new growth model. The majority of the remaining poor population are now living in areas that are frequently destroyed by natural disasters and extreme weather events. These events are projected to become more frequent and severe with climate change. China has become the largest greenhouse gas emitter in the world through its rapid and energy-intensive pattern of growth; therefore, China's future growth model has important implications for global climate change and poverty reduction. The evidence presented in this chapter reaffirms that China must implement more stringent resource and environment-friendly development policies to achieve sustainable poverty reduction through a growth model that is inclusive, pro-poor, green, and environmentally sustainable.

References

Aghion P, Howitt P (1992) A model of growth through creative destruction. Econometrica 60(2):323–351

Amiti M, Freund C (2008) An anatomy of China's export growth. Prepared for 2008 NBER conference

Bardhan P (2009) Economic reforms, poverty and inequality in China and India. Berkley University working paper

Bosworth B, Collins S (2008) Accounting for growth: comparing China and India. J Econ Perspect 22(1):45–66

China National Bureau Statistics (2010) China statistics yearbook 2009. China Statistics Press, Beijing

Chow GC (1993) Capital formation and economic growth in China. Q J Econ 108(3):809–842

Chow GC, Li K-W (2002) China's economic growth: 1952–2010. Econ Dev Cult Change 51(1):247–256

Commissions on Growth and Development (2008) The growth report : strategies for sustained growth and inclusive development. World Bank, Washington, DC

Dean J, Fung KC, Wang Z (2007) Measuring the vertical specialization on Chinese trade. Unpublished mimeo

Dekle R, Vandenbroucke G (2006) A quantitative analysis of China's structural transformation. http://www.frbsf.org/publications/economics/papers/2006/wp06–37bk.pdf

Deng X (1994) Science and technology constitute a primary productive force. In: Works of Deng Xiaoping, vol 3. People's Publishing House, Beijing

Eberhardt M, Helmers C, Yun Z (2011) Is the dragon learning to fly? An analysis of the Chinese patent explosion. CSAE working paper WPS/2011–15, University of Oxford
El-Erian MA, Spence M (2008) Growth strategies and dynamics: insight from country experiences. Commission on Growth and Development, working paper No 6
Fan S, Zhang X (2002) Production and productivity growth in Chinese agriculture: new national and regional measures. Econ Dev Cult Change 50(4):819–838
Fu X (2011) Processing-trade, FDI and exports of indigenous firms: firm-level evidence from high-technology industries in China. Oxford Bull Econ Stat 73(5)
Hofman B, Wu J (2008) Explaining China's development and reforms. Commission on growth and development working paper No 50
Holz CA (2006a) China's reform period economic growth: how reliable are Angus Maddison's estimates? Rev Income Wealth 52(1):85–119
Holz CA (2006b) Measuring Chinese productivity growth, 1952–2005. Unpublished paper. http://ihome.ust.hk/socholz/Chinaproductivity-measures-web-22July06.pdf
Hu Z, Khan M (1997) Why in China growing so Fast. IMF Economic Issues
IMF (2011) People's Republic of China, IMF Country Report No. 11/192
Kanbur R, Squire L (1999) The evolution of thinking about poverty: exploring the interactions. Working papers, Cornell University, Department of Applied Economics and Management
Keefer P (2007) Governance and economic growth. In: Winters A, Yusuf S (eds) Dancing with giants. World Bank/Institute for Policy Studies, Washington, DC/Singapore
Knight J, Ding S (2010) Why does China invest so much? China Growth Centre discussion paper series, no 4
Knight J, Yao Y, Yueh L, Guest Editors (2011) Economic growth in China: productivity and policy editorialintroduction.OxfordBullEconStat73(6):0305-9049.doi:10.1111/j.1468-0084.2011.00679.x
Kuijs L, Wang T (2006) China's pattern of growth: moving to sustainability and reducing inequality. China World Econ 14(1):1–14
Kwan CH (2006) Improving investment efficiency in China through privatization and financial reform. Nomura Capital Mark Rev 9(2):33–43
Lin JY (1992) Rural reforms and agricultural growth in China. Am Econ Rev 82(1)
Lin JY (2012) Demystifying the Chinese economy. Cambridge University Press, Cambridge
Lin Y, Liu Z (2000) Fiscal decentralization and economic growth in China. Econ Dev Cult Change 49(1):1–22
Lin Y, Cai F, Li Z (2003) The China miracle: development strategy and economic reform, Rev. ed. The Chinese University Press, Hong Kong
Naughton B (2006) The Chinese economy: transitions and growth. MIT Press, Cambridge, MA
Riedel J, Jin J, Gao J (2007) How China grows: investment, finance and reform. Princeton University Press, Princeton
Schumpeter JA (1942) Capitalism, socialism and democracy. Harper and Brothers, New York
Sen KA (1999) Development as freedom. Oxford University Press, Oxford
Sen A (2009) Capitalism beyond the crisis. The New York review of books
Wang X (2012) Poverty measurement: theory and methods. Social Sciences Academic Press, Beijing
Wang Y, Yao Y (2003) Sources of China's economic growth 1952–1999: incorporating human capital accumulation. China Econ Rev 14(2003):32–52
World Bank (2009a) Addressing China's water scarcity: recommendations for selected water resource management issues. World Bank, Washington, DC
World Bank (2009b) Good and bad inequality
Zhou Q (2002) Property rights and institutional change. Social Sciences Academic Press, Beijing

Chapter 4
Why China Must Advance Transformation and Improve the Quality of Growth

Throughout history, economic development has always been accompanied by continuous structural transformation underpinned by the process of upgrading endowments (capital, labor, and natural resources), industrial structure, and technology (Lin 2010).[1] Three decades' rapid growth has transformed China from an agriculture-based economy to one dominated by industrial and services sectors, placing China in the ranks of middle-income countries while enabling many people to escape poverty. However, China's growth process, particularly after 2000, has been driven mainly by heavy investment in capital-intensive large-scale industries, infrastructure development, and real estate investment, while consumption growth has been much slower. Such a growth pattern, as put bluntly by Chinese Premier Wen Jiabao, is "unstable, unbalanced, uncoordinated and unsustainable."

Indeed, the growth process over the past decade has exacerbated development imbalances between urban and rural areas and, across regions, generated less employment opportunities and increased income disparity and social insecurity while heightening energy intensity of production and greenhouse gas emissions. China needs to continue to the next stage of economic transformation in order both to sustain its growth and to shift to an inclusive growth pattern that expands employment opportunities more equitably, allowing the majority population to share the benefits of growth. The recent global financial crisis and the consequent and recession in many European countries and the United States, China's major export

[1] The new structural economics approach to sustainable growth proposed by Lin (2010) is centered on three ideas. First, it emphasizes that an economy's structure of factor endowments evolves from one stage of development to another. Second, each stage of economic development is a point along the continuum from a low-income agrarian economy to a high-income industrialized economy, not a dichotomy of two economic development stages ("poor" vs. "rich" or "developing" vs. "industrialized"). Third, at each given stage of development, the market is the basic mechanism for effective resource allocation. However, the government should play an active facilitating role because of the positive externalities of knowledge generation and infrastructure investment in the process of upgrading.

X. Wang et al., *The Quality of Growth and Poverty Reduction in China*,
International Research on Poverty Reduction, DOI 10.1007/978-3-642-36346-7_4,

markets, highlights the risk and vulnerability of China's current unbalanced growth pattern that is driven largely by export, with weak domestic demand.

There are at least four compelling reasons for advocating further structural change of the Chinese economy: (1) the concerns about falling into a "middle-income trap"—a long period of economic stagnation that many Latin American countries experienced in the 1980s and 1990s after reaching middle-income status; (2) the rising income inequality and unbalanced income distribution among the state, enterprises, and households; (3) the structural imbalances both in terms of sectoral composition and among investment, consumption, and net export; and (4) the energy-intensive production patterns and resulting environmental and resource degradation and greenhouse emissions. The issues of income inequality and environmental and resource sustainability will be discussed in Chaps. 4 and 5, respectively. This chapter focuses mainly on the "middle-income trap" and unbalanced macroeconomic structure.

4.1 The Middle-Income Trap

4.1.1 The "Middle-Income Trap"

China's growth pattern during the past decade (2000–2010) has caused much concern about its possible repeating of the "middle-income trap" that many Latin American countries experienced between 1975 and 2000 (see Fig. 4.1). Unlike South Korea which made a timely economic transition from resource-driven growth, with low-cost labor and capital, to a pattern of growth driven by productivity underpinned by technological upgrading and innovation, South Africa, Brazil, and many Latin American countries were caught in the "middle-income trap." Their GDP

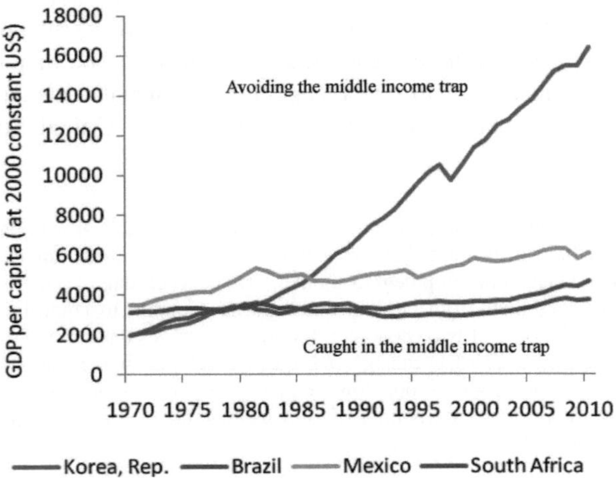

Fig. 4.1 The middle-income trap (*Source:* the World Bank database)

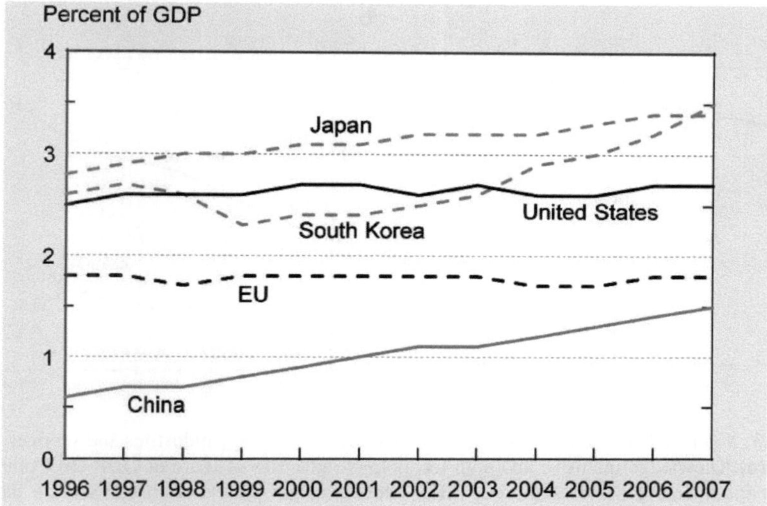

Fig. 4.2 R&D expenditures as percent of GDP: 1996–2007 (*Source*: Organization for Economic Co-operation and Development, Main Science and Technology Indicators (2009/1 and previous years). Science and Engineering Indicators 2010)

growth remained stagnant for several decades because they were unable to compete either with low-income, low-wage economies in manufactured exports or with advanced economies in high-skilled innovations, with their economies characterized by an unbalanced economic structure and high income inequality.

Although China has pursued an export-oriented development path similar to that of Korea during the 1970s–1980s, it has shifted its pattern of growth since the early 2000s, with growth being largely driven by investment in capital-intensive industries, fixed-asset investment, and export. Such a growth pattern is less inclusive in terms of employment creation and also energy intensive, putting pressure on already constrained resources and increasing emissions. In many respects, China's growth pattern over the past decade shares similar characteristics of these countries that fell into the middle-income trap, including rising costs of labor, relying on existing technologies of production rather than homegrown innovations, and rising inequality.

More importantly, while governments in many parts of the world have recognized that advancement in science and technology and innovation, the primary force of production upgrading and structural transformation, must be considered a critical component in economic growth and development, China's growth pattern reflects an inadequate focus on the role of science and technology in driving China's rapid economic expansion. R&D expenditures are long-term investments in innovation and technology development that sustain productivity growth, and many governments set their target at 3 % of GDP devoted to R&D in their efforts to develop knowledge- and technology-based economies (R&D paper 2009). Despite China's rising economic power, its R&D share of GDP was much lower than that in Japan, the United States, and the EU as shown in Fig. 4.2. In contrast, Korea outperformed all other developed countries, in terms of R&D expenditure as a proportion of GDP.

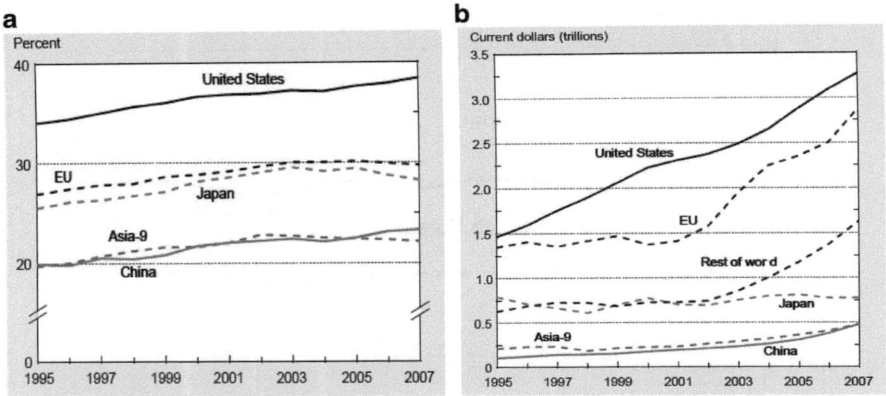

Fig. 4.3 Value added of knowledge-intensive and high-technology industries and services: 1995–2007. (**a**) Knowledge-intensive and high-technology industries as share of GDP. (**b**) Commercial knowledge-intensive services (*Source*: IHS Global Insight, World Industry Service database, Science and Engineering Indicators 2010)

While China is now ranked as the second largest economy in the world, measured by GDP, the country's position in knowledge- and technology-intensive global output has remained relatively small over the past two decades. As shown in Fig. 4.3, the knowledge-intensive and high-technology industries as share of GDP increased moderately, from about 20 % in 1995 to 23 % in 2007, compared with 38 % in the United States, 30 % in the EU, and 27 % in Japan in 2007. Based on the measure of value added by commercial knowledge-intensive services, China also lagged behind. The total value added in commercial knowledge-intensive services increased from about 0.1 (trillions $) in 1995 to only 0.5 (trillions $) in 2007, while the United States and EU increased from 1.5 and 1.4 (trillions $) in 1995, respectively, to 3.2 and 2.8 (trillions $) in 2007, as shown in Fig. 4.3b.

Another important measure of innovation and inventive capacity is the share of patents filed in the US Patent and Trademark Office (USPTO). By this measure, China remained in the 1 % range in all major technology areas throughout the period of 1995–2008, while over 50 % patents filed came from US-based inventors, 20–22 % from Japan, and 14–16 % from the EU. The share of patents filed in USPTO by major Asian countries (excluding China) increased from 4 % in 1995 to about 10 %, largely reflecting patents from Korea inventors, despite its significantly smaller population base. The strong inventive activities in Korea, together with its proportionately large share of R&D expenditure in GDP, may well be one of the key factors that has enabled Korea to maintain its competitiveness once it reached the level of middle-income country and to avoid the middle-income trap.

Although China's future growth pattern will be determined by many factors, both domestically and globally, the concerns about China falling into the "middle-income trap" are justified based on the current pattern of growth, rising income inequality, and relatively weak capacity of science and technology innovation. While China and Korea are not directly comparable, important lessons can be learned from Korea and other Asian countries that avoided the middle-income trap.

4.2 Structural Imbalances

4.2.1 Unbalanced Income Distribution

Three decades' rapid growth has also transformed China from an egalitarian society into one of high inequality. China is now on course to reach the same level of inequality in many Latin American countries, and disparities in key social indicators, such as health and education, are also on the rise. Chapters 4 and 5 provide an in-depth analysis of income inequality and social disparity.

At the national level, the share of income between the three principle economic agents—households, enterprises, and the state—becomes more skewed toward the latter two, with the labor income share in national income shrinking rapidly. The income share of GDP reduced from 51.4 % in 2000 to 45.0 % in 2010, while the government revenue and enterprise profits increased from 14.2 and 34.5 % to 15.2 and 39.7 %, respectively, during the same period. A cross-country comparison of the ratio of labor income and the ratio of tax to GDP shows clearly that while Chinese households were much smaller contributors of national income, the government commands a much larger share of the national income compared with other countries (Fig. 4.4).

The diminished household stake in the national economy is also reflected by the falling share of household consumption in GDP. While many countries in Asia,

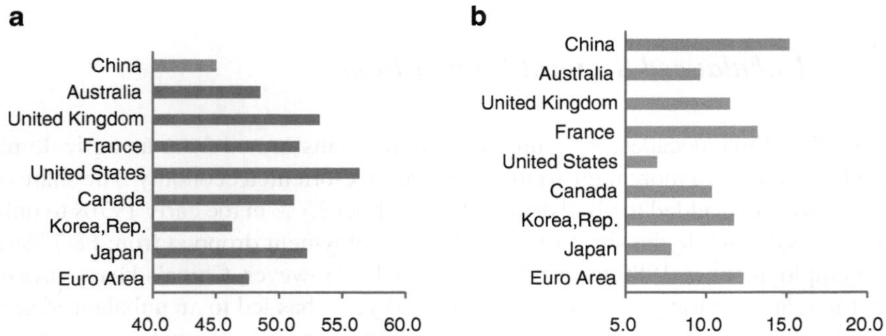

Fig. 4.4 Ratio of labor income and net taxes to GDP in selected countries. (**a**) Ratio of compensation of employees to GDP in selected countries. (**b**) Ratio of net taxes to GDP in selected countries (*Source*: OECD database and China Statistical Yearbook 2011, constructed by authors)

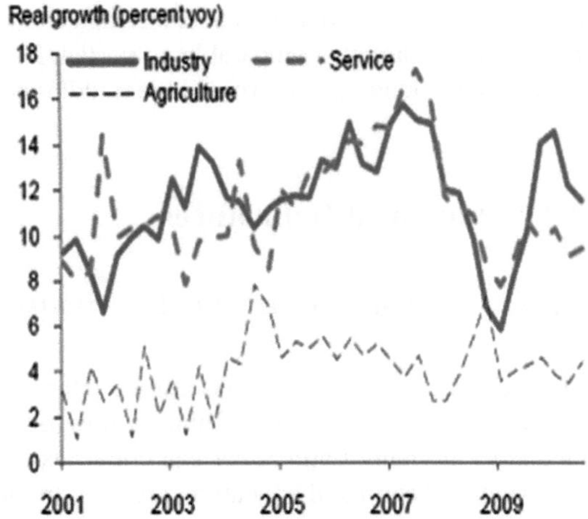

Fig. 4.5 Sectoral growth rate: 1978–2010

including China, Japan, India, Korea, Thailand, Indonesia, Malaysia, Taiwan, and Singapore, all showed a falling trend of the share of consumption in GDP between 1960 and 2008, China is an outlier among Asian countries. Household consumption in China accounts for about 35 % of total GDP, but for all other countries in Asia, the consumption share of GDP ranged between 48 % and 60 % when they were at the same income level as China today (Cui 2010).

The fall in household income as a percentage of GDP reflects the growth pattern that is characterized by a rapid expansion of capital-intensive industries, physical infrastructure, and real estate investment in combination with lagging growth in employment and wages. In reality, the real purchasing power for a majority of Chinese households may have even declined due to the rising cost of living from housing, medical care, and education expenses which were largely provided as part of the social welfare system, in particular in urban areas before 2000.

4.2.2 Unbalanced Sectoral Composition

In less than three decades, the Chinese economy transformed from an agriculture-based economy to a more industrialized and service-oriented economy. The share of agriculture value added to GDP declined from about 35 % in the early 1970s to only 10 % by 2010, while the share of agriculture employment dropped from 68.7 % of total employment in 1980 to just 36.7 % in 2010. However, China's heavy investment in manufacturing sectors over the past 10 years has led to an unbalanced sectoral composition. Since 2009 both industrial and services sectors have witnessed much faster growth than that of agriculture, with the growth rate for industrial sector being 14%, and 10% for services, respectively (see Fig. 4.5).

Table 4.1 International comparison of industrial structure (2008) (%)

	Agriculture	Industry	Services
Low-income countries	25	29	46
Lower-middle-income countries	14	41	45
Middle-income countries	10	37	53
Upper-middle-income countries	6	33	61
High-income countries	1	26	73
China/2010	10.2	46.9	43.0

Note: China's industrial structure refers to the proportions of the primary, secondary, and tertiary industry in GDP
Source: The World Bank: World Bank Development Report 2008. Data for China are from China Statistical Abstract 2011

China's sectoral unbalance is most striking when compared with other middle-income countries. In 2008, in middle-income countries, the average share of the services sector accounted for about 53 % of GDP, but it was only 43 % in China, lower than the low-income country average of 46 % (Table 4.1). The slower growth of the services sector is likely the combination of both investment bias in favor of industries and real estate fixed-assets investment and the shrinking share of labor income in the national economy that determines the growth of services demand, which is largely a non-traded commodity.

4.2.3 Unbalanced Investment and Consumption Growth

China's growth between investment, consumption, and government spending was balanced in the 1990s, but the divergence started in 2000 (Fig. 4.5). While fixed-asset investment surged, the growth of consumption and retail sale lagged behind, and since 2006, the trend of consumption growth has even declined, reflecting the reduced purchasing power from the household sector (see Fig. 4.6). In comparison with Japan, Korea, and Taiwan, although fixed-asset investment grew faster than consumption during their economic booms, consumption still accounted for at least 50 % GDP growth, while in China it was only 26 %.

The scale of China's fixed-asset investment growth over the past three decades was unprecedented, with total fixed-asset investment increasing by 186 times, from RMB 123 billion in 1982 to RMB 22,460 billion in 2009. During this period, the annual growth rate was over 20 %, which is unmatched by any other country in history. Figure 4.6 highlights that China's fixed-asset investment has far surpassed the three most successful economies over the past 50 years—Taiwan, Korea, and Japan—during their respective economic boom years. In 2008, fixed-asset investment accounted for about 40 % of GDP, higher than all other major economies, including Japan (22 %), Germany (19 %), the United States (14 %), Brazil (18 %), and India (39 %)—the world average was 21 % in 2008 (Figs. 4.7 and 4.8).

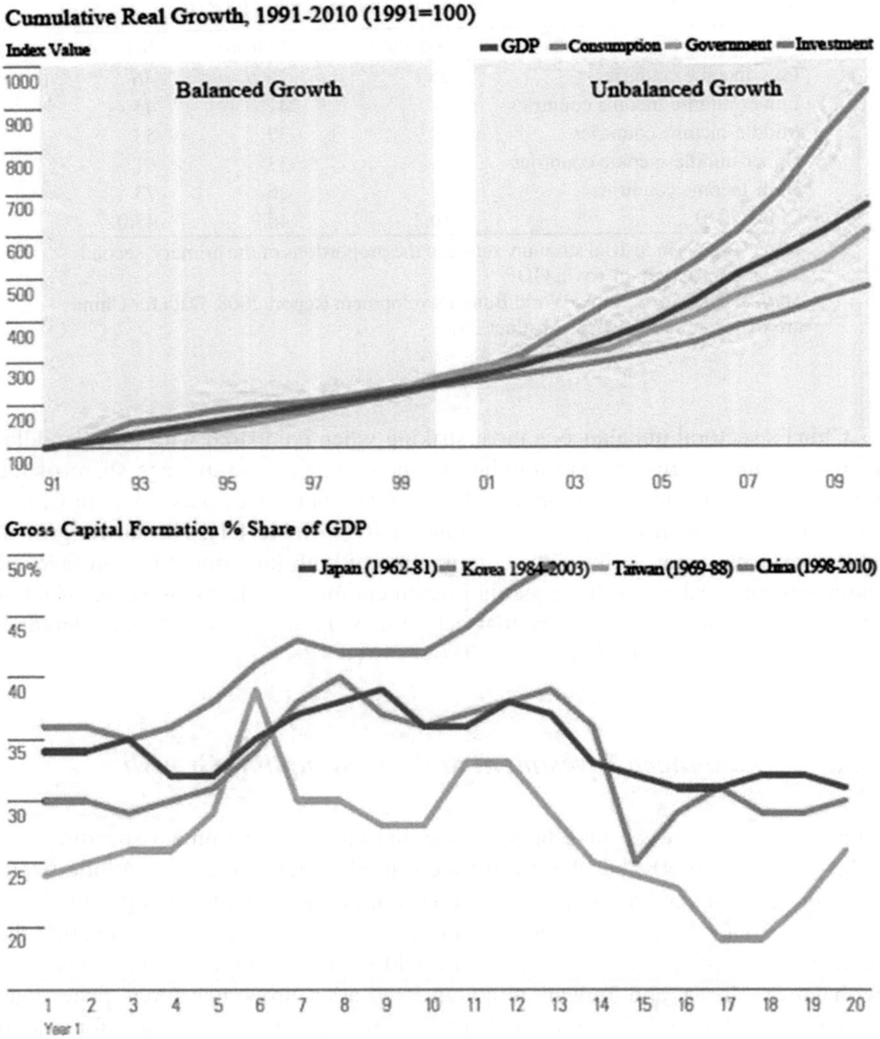

Fig. 4.6 Growth imbalanced: consumption, government, and investment (*Source*: IMF, NBS)

The distribution of fixed-asset investment across industries in 2009 shows that while manufacturing accounted for the largest share of total investment (31 %), the construction and real estate sector came second (21 %), as shown in Fig. 4.9. Fixed-asset investment in the real estate industry grew sharply even after the central government introduced a range of measures in 2010 to prevent the development of a real estate bubble and to curb rising trends in real estate investment (Fig. 4.7). The launch of the stimulus package aimed at mitigating the impact of the 2008 financial crisis increased government-led investment by about 60 % in 2009.

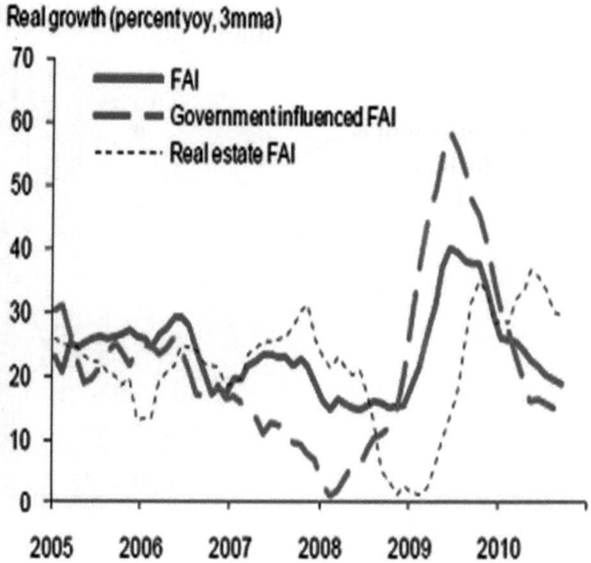

Fig. 4.7 China's fixed-asset investment

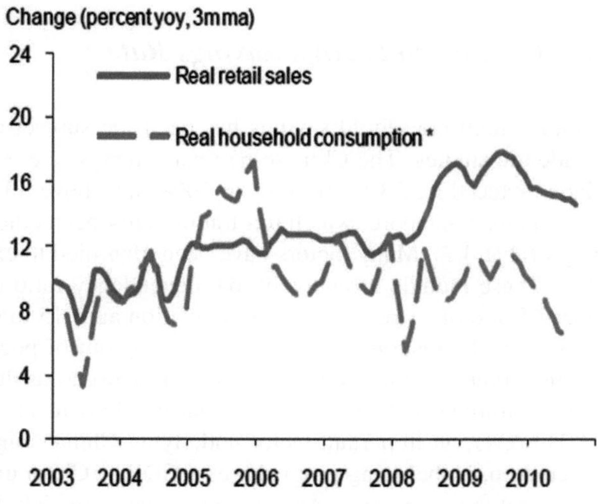

Fig. 4.8 Household consumption and retail sale growth

The overall expansion in construction and real estate development has led to an inevitable property price bubble in China. Given the central position of the property sector in the Chinese economy, which accounted for about 12 % of GDP and 18 % of bank's credit portfolio, and its close linkages with both upstream industries (like steel and cement) and downstream producers of appliances and consumer durable goods, a property bubble could pose a serious risk to macroeconomic and financial sector stability (IMF 2011).

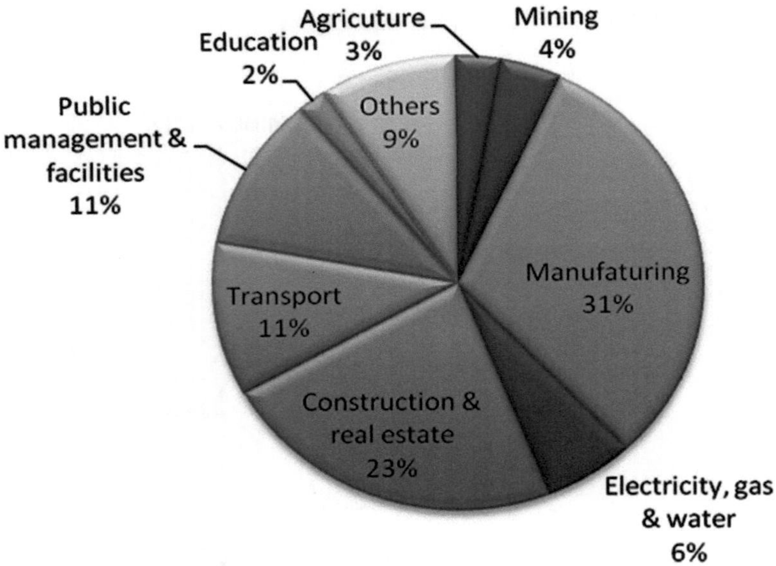

Fig. 4.9 Total fixed-asset investment by industry (2009) (*Source*: http://www.starmass.com/)

4.2.4 Unusually High Savings Rate

China's high household savings has been the subject of much heated debate and academic studies. The Chinese national savings rate is high by international standards, exceeding 53 % of GDP in 2008, far above all the OECD economies and overtaking Singapore, which has traditionally been among the highest savers globally (Table 4.2). Many factors have been identified to explain China's high savings rate. These include a relatively low dependency ratio (the ratio of the population ages 65 and older relative to the population ages 15 to 64), weak social safety net, lack of health insurance coverage and rising out-of-pocket health expenditure, and limited alternative investment options for households due to underdeveloped financial institutions and a government-controlled financial sector.

However, an important factor underlying China's high savings, often omitted in discussion, is the rising profit share in GDP as China undergoes the Lewis dualism structural transformation. As the modern sector (mainly large-sized enterprises) with rising productivity draws surplus labor from the traditional sector, wages have been largely kept below worker's productivity. This is reflected in the declining share of household income in GDP, while the profit share of corporations is rising sharply since 2000. Some even argue that China's weak currency, which makes imports expensive, and its low interest rates on deposits and low lending rates for corporations and developers, are effectively a tax on the household sector (consumption and savings) that transfers incomes from households to the corporate and state sectors.

Table 4.2 Gross national savings: an international perspective (as % of GDP)

	1990	1992	1995	2000	2005	2006	2007	2008
China[1]	39.2	38.8	42.1	36.8	51.2	54.1	54.1	54.3
China[2]	35.6	36.4	38.1	37.3	48.2	49.5	51.8	53.2
Indian	23.0	21.4	24.5	23.8	34.3	35.8	37.6	33.6
Korean	33.2	33.2	29.3	27.5	26.8	26.9	27.0	–
Mexico	37.7	36.9	36.2	33.6	32.7	31.2	30.6	31.9
Singapore	23.6	18.6	21.1	23.8	23.3	25.5	–	–
Australia	43.6	45.8	49.3	46.9	48.7	49.9	51.7	48.3
Canada	18.6	18.0	18.7	19.7	21.6	21.8	22.5	–
France	17.3	13.4	18.3	23.6	23.8	24.4	23.7	–
Germany	20.8	19.6	19.1	21.6	18.5	19.3	19.9	18.9
Italy	25.3	22.3	21.0	20.2	22.2	23.9	25.9	26.0
Switzerland	20.8	19.1	22.0	20.6	19.5	19.6	20.0	18.2
United Kingdom	33.1	28.6	29.6	34.7	36.9	35.5	31.2	–
United States	16.4	14.3	15.9	15.0	14.6	14.2	15.6	–
	15.3	14.2	15.5	17.7	14.6	15.8	14.0	12.1

Note: [1]Expenditure-based estimate of GNS. [2]Production-based estimate of GNS
Data sources: National accounts of OECD countries database; ADB; NSB; authors' own estimates
Source: Ma and Yi (2010)

4.2.5 *Excessive Foreign Exchange Reserve*

China's export-driven growth has reversed the country's position from one with a severe shortage of foreign exchange reserves to being the largest foreign exchange holder in the world. In 2011, China's foreign exchange reserves amounted to $ 3.04 trillion, ranking it first in the world, nearly $2 trillion more than that of Japan, the second largest foreign exchange holder. However, many economists, including Zhou Xiaochuan, the governor of the People's Bank of China, have expressed concerns about China's large accumulation of foreign exchange reserves, which is considered to have far exceeded the level that is compatible with China's stage of development.

Excessively high levels of foreign exchange reserves can lead to excess liquidity and increase the pressure on currency hedging by the Central Bank because of the opportunity cost of holding foreign exchange reserves. Indeed, China has heavily invested much of its foreign exchange reserves in US Treasury securities and other dollar-denominated assets over the past decade. China now is the largest single foreign holder of US government debt, accounting for about 26 % of all foreign-held Treasury securities in 2011. The uncertain prospect of the US debt problems poses a significant risk to China, which may bear massive capital losses, either from the US debt default or from a dollar depreciation if the United States fails to resolve its debt issue.

Table 4.3 Tax revenue structure (2008)

	Items	Revenue (100, million yuan)
Indirect taxes	1. Value-added tax	19,409.7
	2. Consumption tax	2,836.9
	3. Business tax	7,628.4
	4. Tariff	1,770
	5. Resource tax	301.6
	6. Urban maintenance and construction tax	1344.2
	Subtotal	33,290.8 **(60 %)**
Direct taxes	1. Corporate income tax	12,195.2
	2. Individual income tax	3,722.3
	3. Land value increment tax	537.4
	4. Property taxes	551.6
	5. Urban real estate tax	128.7
	6. Urban land use tax	816.9
	7. Arable land occupation tax	314.4
	8. Deed tax	1,307.5
	9. Vehicle and vessel tax	144.2
	10. Tonnage tax	20.1
	11. Stamp duty on securities transactions	1,320.2
	12. Vehicle purchase tax	989.9
	13. Tobacco tax	67.2
	14. Fixed-asset investment orientation regulation tax	1.3
	Subtotal	221,16.9 **(40 %)**
Total taxes		55,407.7 **(100 %)**

Sources: Author's calculation based on China Statistical Yearbooks

4.2.6 Unbalanced Taxation Structure

Since 1995, China has started to modernize its tax system. However, China's taxation structure is not balanced in comparison to more developed economies. Currently, the government derives its tax revenue mainly from indirect taxes (such as value-added tax and other consumption taxes) which account for about 60 % of total tax revenue. The direct tax, in the form of income and property tax, is much lower, amounting to about only 7 % of total revenue in 2008 (Table 4.3).

In comparison, the tax structure in OECD countries relies heavily on income and property tax as the sources of revenue. In 2009, income and property tax accounted about 60–70 % of tax revenue, while indirect tax amounted to 31 % in 2009 (OECD data sources). China's tax structure not only leaves loopholes for tax evasion, it also has limited capacity to function as a redistributive mechanism, which is an important fiscal tool for redistribution in developed economies. Despite China's progressive income tax rate, in many respects, the current tax structure is regressive. This is because while the smaller share of income and property tax in total tax revenue limits its redistributive role, poor households bear a disproportionate burden of consumption tax which dominates the total tax revenue. This conclusion is supported by the findings of Lopez, Thomas, and Wang.

Overall, while China's economic transformation over the past three decades has brought rapid growth and lifted several hundred million people out of poverty through expanded employment opportunities, the pattern of growth over the past decade is unbalanced and unsustainable. The rising income inequality, the global financial crisis and recession in Europe and the United States, as well as the concerns about carbon emissions all reinforce the need for China to advance economic transformation and promote inclusive growth to ensure the benefits of economic expansion are more evenly shared across the population.

The new generation of leaders has realized the problems with China's fiscal system, especially the regressive tax system. Fiscal reforms in improving the collection of direct taxes, including levying the housing property tax, have been implemented widely. In addition, two fiscal structural weaknesses, including the patterns of highly centralized revenue management and decentralized services provision and the consequent heavy reliance of financing through bank borrowing and land development by local government.

Evidence reviewed from this chapter highlights the urgency to reshape policy-making by moving away from a narrow focus on the pace of growth toward an emphasis on the quality of growth. In the next decade, the pattern of growth must rely more on services sector development and less on industries, more productivity growth driven by technological upgrading and innovation and less on capital accumulation, and more on domestic demand and less on net export. Developing national strategies that lead to sustained and inclusive growth ensuring China's next-stage transformation remains a major policy challenge that China must confront in the coming decade.

References

Cui L (2010) China's consumption myth. Hong Kong Monetary Authority working paper. Presentation at the PBoC/IMF Workshop of "Catalyzing Domestic Demand", Beijing, 21 January 2010

IMF (2011) People's Republic of China. IMF country report no. 11/192

Lin YF (2010) The China miracle demystified. Paper prepared for the panel on 'Perspectives on Chinese economic growth' at the Econometric Society World Congress in Shanghai on 19 August 2010

Ma G, Yi W (2010) China's high saving rate: myth and reality. Bank for International Settlement working papers no 312

Chapter 5
Rising Income Inequality

Three decades' rapid growth has transformed China from an egalitarian society into one of alarmingly high inequality, with levels approaching those of Latin American countries. Recent history shows that inequality can be a root cause of social unrest and seriously undermine the political legitimacy of governments. The Chinese government rightly places the issue of inequality at the top of its policy agenda and has recently introduced a wide range of measures to address inequality.

In addition to the social and political concerns of inequality, the relationship between growth and income inequality has occupied a central place in economic policy debates for over 50 years since the pioneering work of Kuznets (1955). However, the relationship between growth and income inequality is still controversial. Its controversy lies in the difficulties of reconciling the different theories and in the inconclusiveness of empirical evidence.[1] But despite the controversy, it is widely accepted that an economy's growth rate and its income distribution are both

[1] As reviewed by Lundberg and Squire (2003), the empirical literature has evolved in one of two directions. One line of research follows in the tradition of Kuznets and focuses on the question of whether more inequality enhances or inhibits the growth rate. This is addressed by running regressions of growth rates on measures of inequality and examining the signs of the relevant regression coefficients. Tests of this hypothesis by Anand and Kanbur (1993), Alesina and Rodrik (1994), Persson and Tabellini (1994), Perotti (1996), and others obtain a negative relationship. The various explanations for this include the political economy consequences of inequality (Alesina and Rodrik), the fact that inequality may harm education (Galor and Zeira 1993), and the unequal distribution of natural resources (Gylfason and Zoega 2003). Other studies find a positive, or at least more ambiguous, relationship; see, e.g., Li and Zou (1998), Forbes (2000), and Barro (2000). In particular, Barro finds a negative relationship between inequality and growth for poorer countries, but a positive relationship in the case of richer countries. The second approach involves examining the determinants of growth and inequality as essentially independent processes. Lundberg and Squire (2003) introduce a number of factors that may potentially influence both inequality and growth and test for their joint significance. They identify two factors (measures of civil liberty and openness) that are likely to impact both variables in the same direction, thereby implying a positive relationship between income inequality and growth. Deininger and Squire (1996) conclude that the fear that economic growth on its own will have a systematic negative effect on the distribution of income is unfounded.

X. Wang et al., *The Quality of Growth and Poverty Reduction in China*,
International Research on Poverty Reduction, DOI 10.1007/978-3-642-36346-7_5,

endogenous outcomes of the economic system. Therefore, both outcomes are subject to common influences, in particular structural changes and macroeconomic policies.

The central message of the Kuznets curve is that income inequality dynamics and growth are intimately connected when countries are undergoing a structural transformation to become industrialized economies. Therefore, rising income inequality should be viewed as part of a wider process of economic growth and transformation. A sensible approach to assess China's growth patterns should focus on the inclusiveness of the growth process, in addition to the income distribution dimension of the growth process, which has been overly emphasized in the pro-poor growth literature (for detailed discussion, see Appendix 2).[2] Therefore, a more important question is whether the growth process is inclusive—whether the majority of the Chinese population participated in the growth process through expanded job opportunities. In answering this question, a sound understanding of the key features of rising income inequality as well as the sources of rising inequality is essential.

5.1 Key Features of Income Equality

Inequality in China has risen sharply since the beginning of the economic reform in 1978. This rising trend of income inequality is confirmed using various measures and data sources. Figure 5.1 shows that the Gini index increased sharply from the

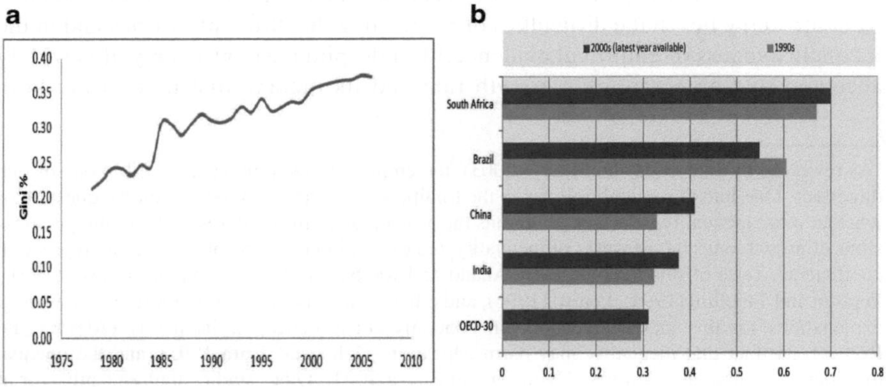

Fig. 5.1 Trend of inequality: 1975–2006. (**a**) Gini coefficient. (**b**) Gini coefficient of household income (*Source:* National submissions for Brazil, India, and South Africa. WDI for China and OECD-30)

[2] In fact, by narrowly focusing on inequality, it is possible to lead to suboptimal outcomes for both poor and nonpoor households. For example, a growth pattern characterized with low income inequality (e.g., an average income growth of 2 % while the income of poor households grew by 3 %) is less inclusive and inferior to a growth pattern of higher inequality (e.g., the average growth rate was 6 %, but the income of poor households grew by only 4 %) (Ianchovichina and Lundstrom 2009).

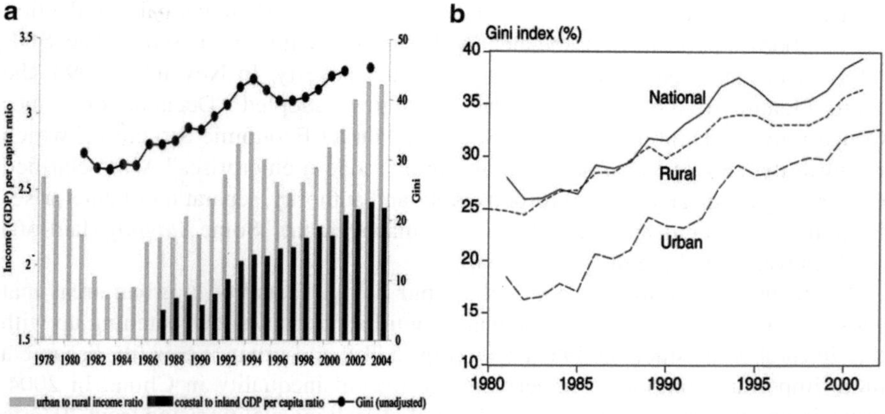

Fig. 5.2 Inequality. (**a**) Trends of income inequality in China (*Source*: Huang and Luo 2008). (**b**) Inequality: rural, urban, and total (*Source*: Chen and Ravallion)

mid-1980s until 1985 when rural income growth started to slow down as a result of the shifting focus of development policies to the urban industrial sector and coastal regions. Compared with other large developing economies and OECD countries, China experienced the largest increase in inequality between the 1990s and 2000s.

The overall inequality in China was manifested in the regional disparity and rural-urban divide, as summarized in Fig. 5.2, although in recent years, the rapid rising inequality in urban areas has also started to cause concern, as shown in Fig. 5.2b. The regional development gap is most evident between coastal and inland regions. The coastal to inland GDP per capita ratio rose from 1.7 in the late 1980s to 2.4 in 2004 (Huang and Luo 2008), reaching the highest level in a half-century (Kanbur and Zhang 1999).

The growing concern about the spatial dimension of inequality is not unique to China. In Russia, India, Mexico, and South Africa, as well as most other developing and transition economies, various measures show that spatial and regional disparities in economic activity, incomes, and social indicators are on the rise (Kanbur and Venables 2005). In China, regional inequality can become particularly concerning when regional divisions serve a potential source of political and ethnic tensions that undermine social and political stability.

In contrast to regional income disparity, rural-urban inequality had evolved differently since the start of the economic reform. While the rural-urban gap was on a rising trend, Fig. 5.2b shows there are two periods of substantial reduction in rural-urban income disparity: (1) between 1978 and the mid-1980s and (2) the period between the mid-1990s and late 1990s. Both were closely associated with the introduction of economic reform programs and various social policies. The first episode of the decline in rural-urban income inequality was largely a result of the introduction of the rural household responsibility system in 1978, and the agricultural pricing policy that raised food-grain procurement prices, together with policy changes that allowed farmers to sell agricultural products at much higher prices in urban areas. The second period of rural-urban inequality reduction (1994–2000) was closely associated with the restructuring of SOEs. The SOE reform had increased urban unemployment and poverty. In November 1993, the Third Plenum of the Fourteenth Party Congress adopted "Decision on Issues Concerning the Establishment of a Socialist Market Economic Structure," which set forth the task of transforming SOEs into "modern enterprises" with "clarified property rights, clearly defined responsibility and authority, separation of enterprises from the government, and scientific internal management." Some *Xiagang* (laid-off) workers were caught in the poverty trap.

In recent years, however, it was the rapid rising inequality in urban areas that caused a major public concern. Inequality in urban areas was fast catching up with that in rural areas since the late 1990s (Fig. 5.2b), and urban inequality became a more important component underlying the overall inequality in China. In 2004, urban inequality accounted for about 36 % of overall inequality, rising from 20 % in 1989 (Luo and Zhu 2008).

The rising urban inequality warrants special policy attention for two reasons. First, the significant political stake that the urban population commands in Chinese society means a sharp rising inequality in urban areas can potentially lead to political and social instability. Secondly, the continuous massive inflow of rural migrants into urban areas is likely to further aggravate inequalities and poverty in urban areas if measures are not in place to facilitate rural-urban migration by providing basic social services and equal legal rights to the migrants.

Indeed, many inequality studies cover only the officially defined urban population, excluding rural-urban migrants who reside in urban areas almost permanently. Evidence based on targeted surveys shows that the average income of migrants is much lower than that of urban residents; the average hourly wage for migrants was about 9.8 (RMB), compared with 13.5 (RMB) for urban residents in 2010 (Cai et al. 2011). In addition, income inequality among migrants was much higher, with the Gini coefficient of hourly income at 0.42 for migrants, compared with 0.38 for their urban counterparts (Lewei Zhang 2011). This suggests that urban inequality is likely to be much higher when taking into account migrant populations.

5.2 Sources of Rising Income Inequality

As China was deepening its economic and structural transformation, rising income inequality was inevitable. Five decades ago, Lewis made it clear "development must be inegalitarian because it does not start in every part of the economy at the same time." A more important question concerns what is driving China's rapidly increasing income equality.

First, on the spatial income disparity in China, in particular, between the coastal and inland regions. The dramatic increase in income disparity between coastal China and the interior is likely a combination of differential geographic conditions and government preferential industrial policies. The coastal provinces enjoyed geographic advantages in terms of proximity to ports and the closer links with the

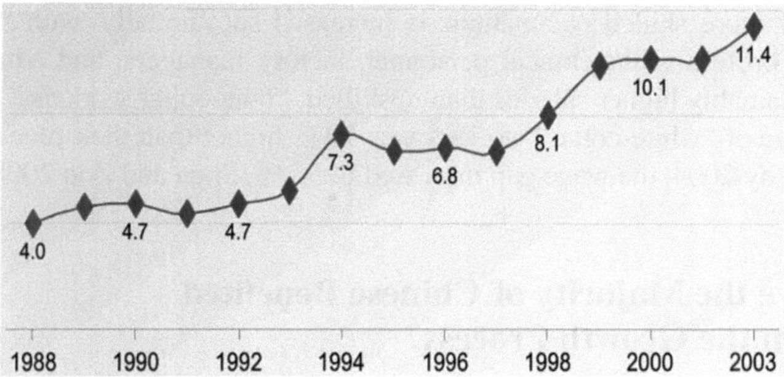

Fig. 5.3 Annual returns to schooling in urban areas as % of annual wages (*Source*: Zhang et al. 2005)

Newly Industrialized Economies, such as Hong Kong, South Korea, Taiwan, and Singapore. In addition, the labor force in coastal regions is relatively more educated. For example, the average years of formal education of the working age population were 5.9 in coastal rural areas, compared with 5.2 inland in 1989, although disparity in education attainment among the urban population was negligible (Luo and Zhu 2008).

The government preferential industrial policies also contribute to income disparity between coastal and inland regions. In 1989, as the first step of its large-scale open-door policies, the government introduced special economic zones aimed at opening up coastal regions to international trade and attracting FDI. The openness to international trade and massive inflow of FDI no doubt played an important role in raising incomes in coastal regions at a much faster rate than in the rest of China.

The economic success in coastal China, to some extent, is consistent with the theory of "second nature geography." It argues that openness to international trade creates the forces of agglomeration that lead to concentration of economic activity, bringing the benefits of returns to scale.[3] In turn, these forces generate virtuous circles of self-reinforcing economic growth in coastal regions, which drive spatial income disparity.

Second, the significant increase in return to education is another major factor underlying rising inequality in China. The increasing dominance of the private sector in China's overall economy, together with the restructuring of SOEs, intensifies competition among firms. In order to maintain competitiveness, firms strive to continuously improve efficiency, upgrade production through new investment, and compete for more educated and skilled workers.

The economic reform has created a labor market where wage returns to education have been substantially increased. For example, the wage return to one additional year of schooling increased from 4 % in 1988 to 11 % in 2003 (Fig. 5.3). Similarly, the wage

[3] A considerable branch of the long-run growth literature argues for both direct and indirect effects of geography on development (McArthur and Sachs 2001; Bloom and Sachs 1998; Sachs 2001). Rodrik et al. (2004) and Acemoglu et al. (2001, 2002) show that geography only indirectly affects growth through institutions, but these indirect effects are very large.

premium of more skilled occupations is increased substantially, with "white-collar jobs" (e.g., professional/technical personnel, factory managers, and administrators), earning sustainably higher salaries than unskilled, "blue-collar workers." In 1989, the average wage of "white-collar" workers was 10 % higher than their blue-collar counterparts, but by 2004, the wage gap increased to 55 % (Shen and Zou 2008).

5.3 Have the Majority of Chinese Benefited from the Growth Process?

The patterns and sources of rising income inequality, together with the phenomenal reduction in poverty, show clearly that the masses were able to participate in and benefit from the economic growth, in particular before the early 2000s. Indeed, to a great extent, the majority of people benefited from economic growth, although not evenly across the spectrum of the population. In this respect, the pattern of growth was, by and large, an inclusive process enabling the majority of Chinese to benefit from the expanded productive employment opportunities brought about by economic growth.

A large body of empirical studies on inequality and growth in China provides strong evidence that supports such conclusions. For example, evidence from a large-scale household survey covering 8 provinces, including three coastal provinces (Jiangsu, Shandon, and Liaoning) and five inland provinces (Henan, Hubei, Hunan, Guangxi, and Guizhou), shows that in the coastal regions where the economic growth was faster than that of the interior, the entire rural population experienced a large increase in income between 1989 and 2004 (Luo and Zhu 2008). In particular, the poorest and richest segments of the rural population registered the largest increase in household income as reflected in the U-shaped growth incidence curve shown in Fig. 5.4 (a technical note on the growth incidence curve is presented in Appendix 2).

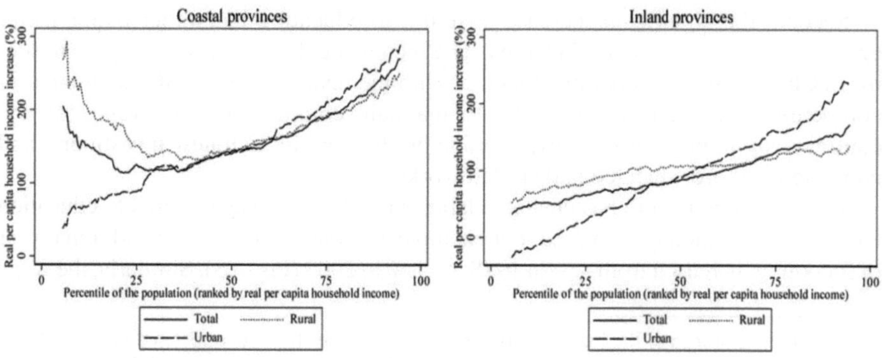

Fig. 5.4 Inclusive growth: growth incidence curve (*Source*: Luo and Zhu 2008)

In urban areas, the bottom income groups in more dynamic coastal regions also experienced an increase in income, although much less than the top income groups. In contrast, in the relatively stagnant inland provinces, urban households saw a decrease in income during the survey period between 1989 and 2004 (see Fig. 5.4).

The expansion of employment opportunities, in particular in the dynamic coastal regions, was the major principal factor underlying the income increase for both the poor and better-off households. The productivity growth in the agricultural sector and a series of rural sector reform policies introduced since the early 1980s made it possible to release a large pool of surplus rural laborers who were subsequently absorbed into the rural nonfarming sector through the rapid expansion of rural industries, such as TVEs, and other high-return off-farming activities. Later, these laborers became the major workforce employed in the rapidly growing export sector, dominated by labor-intensive manufacturing industries in coastal regions.

In addition, many rural residents increased their incomes from new employment opportunities in large cities nearby, such as Shanghai for Jiangsu and Bohai Economic Zone for Shandong and Liaoning (Luo and Zhu 2008). These expanded employment opportunities helped hundreds and thousands of people move out of poverty during the past few decades of fast economic growth.

In many respects, the growing income inequality in China over the past few decades reflects the rising importance of the middle class which did not exist before the early 1980s. In the 1990s, the average annual growth in real household income for the bottom 20 %, middle 20 %, and top 20 % was 3.6 %, 6.4 %, and 8.7 %, but it increased to 8.5 %, 11.4 %, and 15.1 %, respectively, in the 2000s (OECD 2010). The per capita income share of the middle 60 % of the population increased sharply during the past two decades. In 2008, the middle 60 % population accounted for about 55 % of total income, while the top quintile (20 %) accounted for 40 %, which is similar to the share observed in the OECD countries in the mid-2000s (Fig. 5.5).

The rising income inequality reflects a growth pattern that has become more capital intensive and less inclusive in terms job creation in recent years. Before 1993, China's growth was accompanied by employment growth averaging 5.4 %, a figure comparable with those of other countries in Asia. In the early 1990s, however, the trends between the growth of fixed capital accumulation (as % of GDP) and the employment growth (total employment in both industrial and services sectors) started to diverge (see Fig. 5.6).

Since 1993, despite the rapid growth in fixed capital formation and export growth, the growth in employment declined. The employment growth rate in the industrial sector reduced to about 2.1 % in 2000, from over 5 % during 1980–1999, and slid to negative levels in 2002 (−3.1 %), before picking up again from 2007 onward. Clearly, the pattern of capital-intensive growth since the early 2000s was less conducive to job creation. Overall, China's growth process was inclusive, in particular, during the first two decades, but becoming less so in the past 10 years. The rising returns to education and skills indicate that disadvantaged populations, including the less educated and rural populations, were most likely excluded disproportionally from the growth process in recent years, which may have exacerbated income inequality.

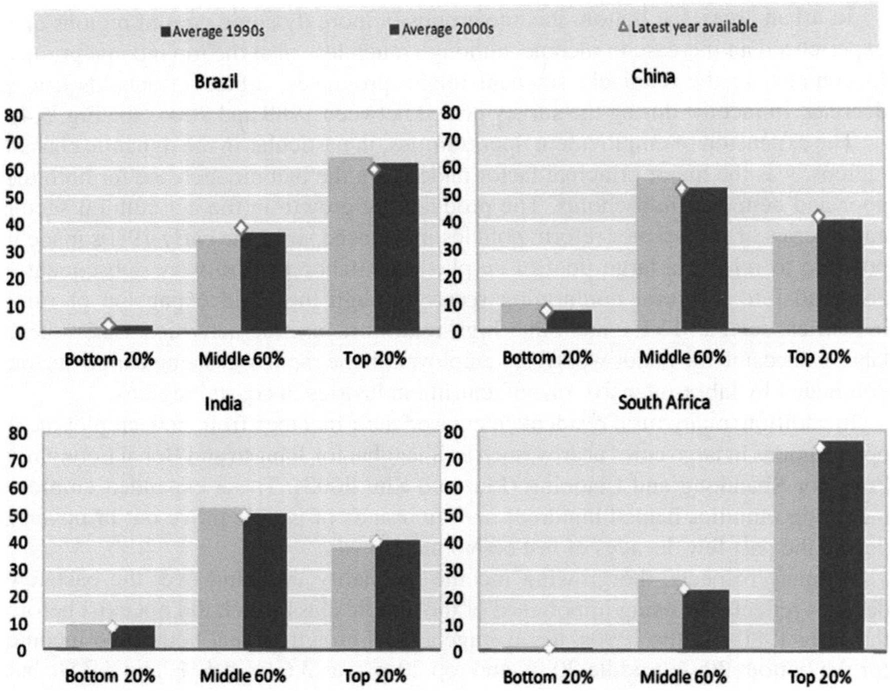

Fig. 5.5 Per capita income shares by quintile (%) (*Source*: National submissions based on PNAD for Brazil, NSS for India and SALDRU 1993, IES 2000 and NIDS 2008 for South Africa. For China data come from the Milanovic database)

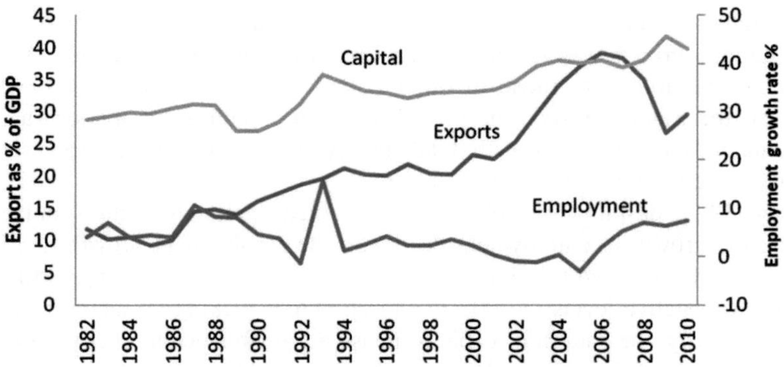

Fig. 5.6 Fixed capital investment and employment growth trends (*Source*: Author's calculation based on China Statistical Yearbooks)

References

Acemoglu D, Johnson S, Robinson J (2001) The colonial origins of comparative development: an empirical investigation. Am Econ Rev 91:1369–1401
Acemoglu D, Johnson S, Robinson J (2002) Reversal of fortune: geography and institutions in the making of the modern world income distribution. Q J Econ 117(4):1231–1294
Alesina A, Rodrik D (1994) Distributive politics and economic growth. Q J Econ 109:465–490
Anand S, Kanbur SMR (1993) The Kuznets process and the inequality-development relationship. J Dev Econ 40:25–52
Barro RJ (2000) Inequality and growth in a panel of countries. J Econ Growth 5(1):5–32
Bloom DE, Sachs JD (1998) Geography, demography, and economic growth in Africa. Brook Pap Econ Act 1988(2):207–295
Cai F, Du Y, Wang M (2011) Rural labour migration and poverty reduction in China. IPRCC working paper series, No 7. IPRCC, Beijing
Deininger K, Squire L (1996) Measuring income inequality: a new data base. World Bank Econ Rev 10:565–591
Forbes K (2000) A reassessment of the relationship between inequality and growth. Am Econ Rev 90:869–887
Galor O, Zeira J (1993) Income distribution and macroeconomics. Rev Econ Stud 60:35–52
Gylfason T, Zoega G (2003) Inequality and growth: do natural resources matter? In: Eicher TS, Turnovsky SJ (eds) Inequality and growth: theory and policy implications. MIT Press, Cambridge, MA
Huang Y, Luo K (2008) Reshaping economic geography: the China experience. In: Huang Y, Magnoli Bocchi A (eds) Reshaping economic geography in East Asia. World Bank, Washington, DC
Ianchovichina E, Lundstrom S (2009) Inclusive growth analysis: framework and application, World Bank Policy Research working paper, 4851. World Bank, Washington, DC
Kanbur R, Venables AJ (2005) Spatial inequality and development. Oxford University Press, Oxford/New York
Kanbur R, Zhang X (1999) Which regional inequality? The evolution of rural-urban and inland-coastal inequality in China, 1983–1995. J Comp Econ 27:686–701
Kuznet S (1955) Economic growth and income inequality. Am Econ Rev 65:1–28
Lewei Zhang (2011) Income inequality in Urban China: a comparative analysis between urban residents and rural-urban migrants, working paper. The Sanford School of Public Policy, Duke University
Li HY, Zou HF (1998) Income inequality is not harmful to growth: theory and evidence. Rev Dev Econ 2:318–334
Lundberg M, Squire L (2003) The simultaneous evolution of growth and inequality. Econ J 113(487):326–344
Luo X, Zhu N (2008) Rising income inequality in China: a race to the top, The World Bank Policy Research working paper, 4700. World Bank, Washington, DC
OECD Secretariat (2010) Growth, employment and inequality in Brazil, China India and South Africa: an overview. OECD Secretariat, Paris
Perotti R (1996) Growth, income distribution, and democracy: what the data say. J Econ Growth 1:149–187
Persson T, Tabellini G (1994) Is inequality harmful for growth? Am Econ Rev 84:600–621
Rodrik D, Subramanian A, Trebbi F (2004) Institutions rule: the primacy of institutions over geography and integration in economic development. J Econ Growth 9:131–165
Sachs JD (2001) Tropical underdevelopment, NBER working paper, no. 8119. National Bureau of Economic Research, Cambridge, MA. http://www.nber.org/papers/w8119
Shen C, Zou H (2008) China: regional disparities in poverty distribution. Div Labor Trans Costs (DLTC) 3(01):17–56, World Scientific Publishing Co. Pte. Ltd
Zhang J, Zhao Y, Parl A, Song X (2005) Economic returns to schooling in urban China, 1988–2001. J Comp Econ 33:730–752

Chapter 6
Social Disparity and Inequality of Opportunity

In *Development as Freedom*, Sen (1999) emphasizes that development must be focused on individual entitlements, capabilities, freedom, and rights and that economic growth is the means to these ends. In this approach, expansion of freedom is viewed as both the *primary end* and the *principal means* of economic development. It is essential to ensure basic income so that people may be free from poverty and hunger, to provide access to basic health care so that people may live a long and healthy life, and to afford access to education so that people may realize their aspirations. People are both the beneficiaries of development and the agents of the progress and changes that development brings about. This means issues of equity must be central to economic development. The notion of equity includes both income and human capabilities, such as health and education outcomes, equality of opportunities, and gender equality.

However, judged by the notion of development advocated by Sen, China's economic growth process in recent years, in many aspects, falls short of what constitutes development. Before the 1970s, China was able to achieve impressive health and education outcomes, with a very low level of income (Fig. 6.1). The average life expectancy in China was 67 in the 1980s, about 10 years higher than the average in low-income countries. Women enjoyed significant equality with men in many social dimensions compared with countries at a similar stage of development. The female adult literacy rate reached 51 % and life expectancy was 69 in the early 1980s, development indicators surpassing those in many middle-income countries.[1]

However, as China experienced the fastest growth in history, the national health performance has not fared well, even witnessing a slowdown of health gains. China has regressed from an outstanding performer (measured by impressive health outcomes relative to income levels) to an average performer in the cross-country comparison between the two periods of 1970–1974 and 1995–1999 (Fig. 6.1). While income inequality was rising sharply in China, disparities in health and education

[1] The comparison between China and India is most telling: in China, over 45 % of female adults were literate and the female labor participation rate was over 70 % in the 1980s, compared with 25 % and 32 %, respectively, in India during the same period.

X. Wang et al., *The Quality of Growth and Poverty Reduction in China*, International Research on Poverty Reduction, DOI 10.1007/978-3-642-36346-7_6,

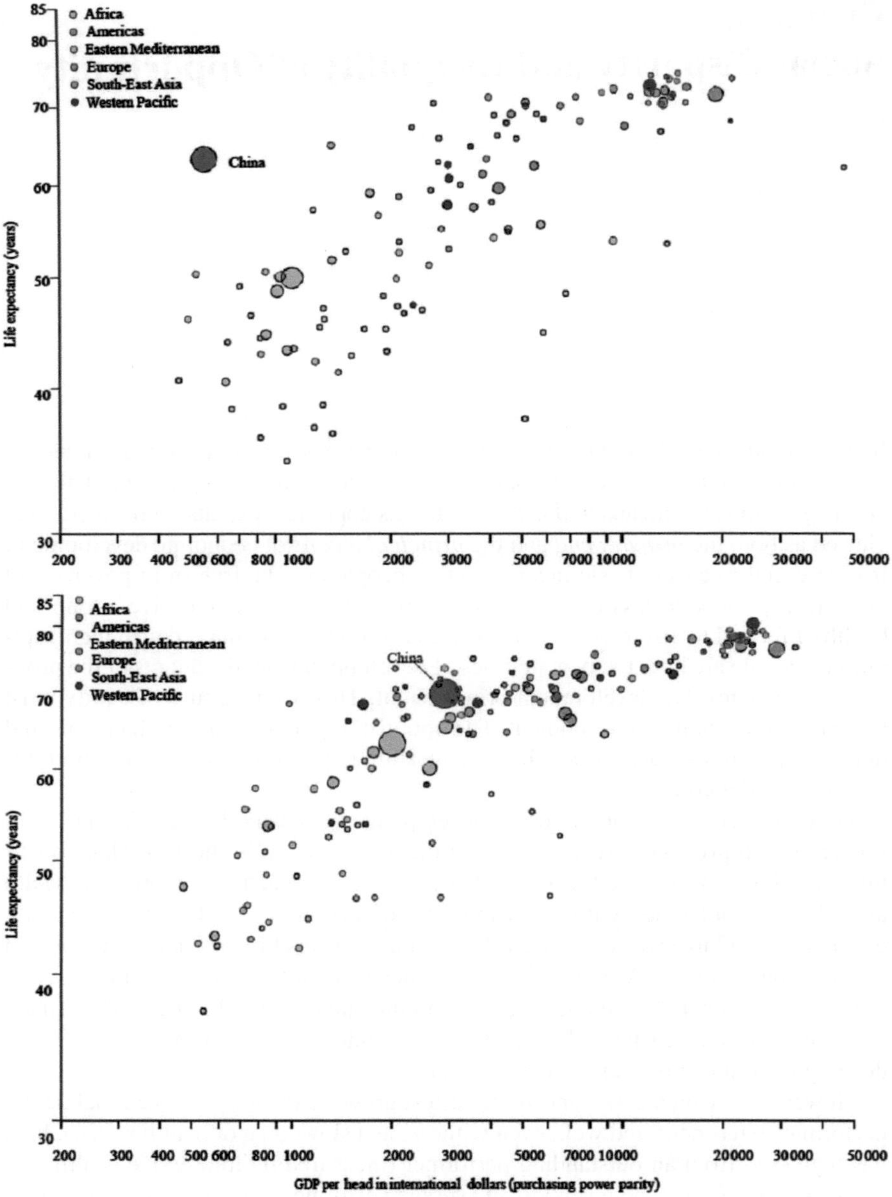

Fig. 6.1 Trends in national life expectancy by GDP per capita for selected countries in 1970–1974 (*top*) and 1995–1999 (*bottom*) (*Source*: Tang et al. 2008)

between urban and rural areas, across region and socioeconomic groups, both in terms of access and outcomes, were also widening.

This chapter examines the progress of social outcomes in the course of China's three decades of economic growth and reform, focusing on the role of government in social services provision, disparities in health and education, and gender equality.

6.1 The Shrinking Role of Government in Social Services Provision

While China's economic power, measured by GDP and government revenue, is accelerating, the role of government in the provision of basic social services is shrinking rapidly. Unlike the situation in many countries that are ridden by economic recession and mounting government budget deficit, China's economic growth has significantly strengthened its fiscal capacity. The government revenue increased from RMB 315 billion in 1991 to RMB 6,852 billion in 2007, reflecting a 22 times increase during this period.

Although official government spending overall has increased in China—from 17.7 % of GDP in 1995 to 20.8 % of GDP in 2008—it is still well below the OECD average of 44.5 %. This acceleration in public spending, however, has been most marked in infrastructure investment and public administration, not in the area of health and education (OECD Report 2007). Public spending on health and education amounted to the equivalent of 3 % of GDP in 2008, much lower compared with the OECD level of over 30 % in the same year (OECD, StatExtracts). The government's contribution to health-care financing also declined sharply during this period as shown in Fig. 6.2. This is in sharp contrast with OECD countries, where, in 2010,

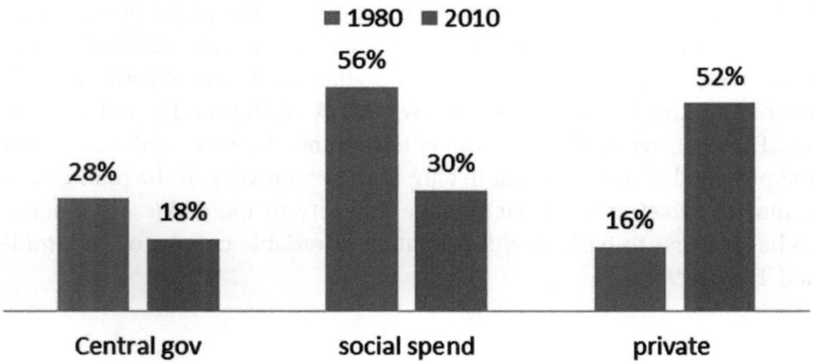

Fig. 6.2 Health spending by source: 1980 vs. 2010 (*Source:* Authors' construction based on China Statistical Yearbooks)

the share of public spending in total health expenditure was 76 % while private sources contributed 24 %.

China's highly decentralized fiscal system further aggravates social disparity. With local governments responsible for funding local services, poor regions were not able to provide quality basic social services, and poor households could not afford the high private costs of health and education services. Consequently, rising income inequality reinforced inequality in social indicators.

6.2 Disparity in Health and Education

While China had made great strides in improving population health outcomes over the past two decades, progress was uneven. First, within China, improvement in life expectancy has been much slower in poor provinces than in rich ones. In Shanghai, the richest city in China, life expectancy was 78 years in 2000, but in the poorest provinces, it was 65 years—a gap of 13 years is striking in comparison with the United States and the United Kingdom. In 2001–2003, the gap in life expectancy between the US states with the highest (Minnesota) and lowest (District of Columbia) life expectancy was 6.5 years.[2] In the United Kingdom, among the 12 regions and counties, the life expectancy gap in 2004–2006 was 2.6 years for men and 2.7 years for women.[3]

Second, the gap in mortality rates between rural and urban areas is also widening. A recent study by UNICEF shows that maternal and child mortality rates in poor rural areas are 4–6 times higher than those in urban areas, with poor rural areas accounting for 70–75 % of all maternal and child deaths in 2004. The majority of maternal and child deaths are caused by a few preventable conditions,[4] suggesting a lack of access to basic health-care services being the major factor underlying the disparity in rural-urban mortality rates.

The transition to a market economy eroded the widespread provision of basic social services that was achieved during the pre-reform era as a result of government-led investment in public services. Before the economic reform in 1978, the Cooperative Medical Scheme covered over 90 % of the rural population in China (Liu et al. 1998), while the Government Insurance Scheme and Labor Insurance Scheme provided almost free health care to the employees of the public sector and institutions in urban areas. Basically, the majority of the Chinese population was able to have access to basic health care at an affordable cost before the mid-1980s (Gu and Tang 1995).

[2] US Census Bureau and Population Division (2005).

[3] Office for National Statistics. Life expectancy at birth and at age 65 by local areas in the United Kingdom.

[4] The leading causes of death include postpartum hemorrhage, hypertension, and embolism for maternal deaths and neonatal trauma, preterm delivery, and low birth weight for child deaths.

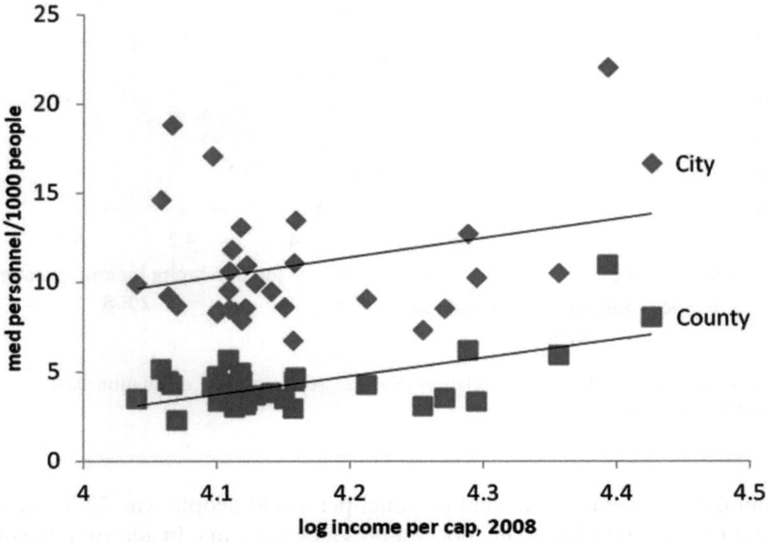

Fig. 6.3 Medical technical personnel (*Source*: Authors' own estimation based on China Statistical Yearbooks)

China's market-driven reform reversed this situation. The Cooperative Medical Scheme collapsed in most rural areas following de-collectivization. Less than 10 % of the rural population was covered by insurance schemes from the late 1980s to 2000 (Tang et al. 2008). The most disadvantaged rural populations became more vulnerable to health shocks, which were the leading cause of poverty in rural areas.

In urban areas, a new Urban Employee Basic Health Insurance Scheme has been developed to replace the Government Insurance Scheme and Labor Insurance Scheme. However, the newly established insurance scheme was designed with a strong emphasis on profit-making, partially in response to the declining role of government in health-care financing, thus leading to a rapid escalation in health-care costs in the past decade.[5] Together with the lack of health insurance, hospital care became unaffordable to a majority of rural residents. The average patient has to pay out-of-pocket 60 % of the cost of a hospital visit, compared with 25 % in Mexico, 10 % in Turkey, and a much lower amount in most developed countries (Dollar 2007).

The gap in access to basic health services has widened between rural and urban areas, as well as between rich and poor provinces—richer provinces retain many more medical personnel per 1,000 residents (see Fig. 6.3). In rural areas, access to health-care services declined over time; in 1980, the total number of village doctors per 1,000 people was 1.81, but this number fell to 1.06 in 2008. In 2008, the

[5] The health sector reform distorted the incentives of health-care providers, encouraging hospitals to recover costs through high fees on drugs and undertaking expensive medical procedures while reducing the supply of preventive care services.

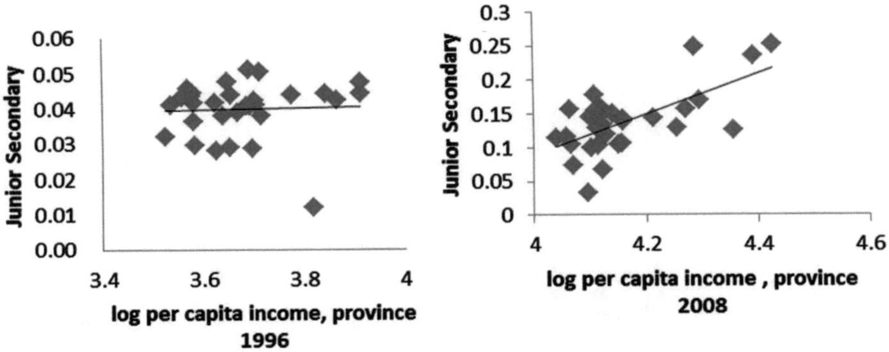

Fig. 6.4 Education and income correlation (*Source:* Authors' own estimation based on China Statistical Yearbooks)

total number of technical medical personal per 1,000 people was 22.3 in Beijing, compared with 9.9 in Gansu, the poorest province in China. In addition, the quality of health services in poor areas is much lower, as township hospitals, the primary health providers for rural populations, have far less facilities and qualified medical personnel than urban areas. Amid China's economic miracle, disparities in access to basic health care and in health outcomes increased and, in recent years, the progress made to overall improvement of health has become stagnant.

The trend in education disparities is similar to that in health. While significant progress has been made in raising overall education attainment since the early 1980s, disparity in education outcomes is increasing. Up through the 1990s, there was little difference in school attainment rates across provinces, but by 2008 a strong positive association between the school attainment rate and income emerged (see Fig. 6.4). Children from rich provinces are more likely to progress to junior high school than their counterparts from poor provinces, with the average junior high school enrolment rate around 12 % in poor provinces, but over 25 % in the rich ones in 2008.

The rapid increase in income, together with the reduced role of government in education financing, also spurred the development of private sector education. Increasingly, better-off households send their children to private schools which are equipped with better facilities and higher-quality teaching staff, while many public schools are struggling to recruit qualified teachers. For example, in 2007, substitute or part-time teachers with less qualifications accounted for more than 94 % of the total teaching staff in rural and township schools (UNDP 2005).

The dramatic increase in return to education, one of the positive developments in China's economic transition, creates strong incentives for families to investment in their children's education. However, if only the better-off households can investment in their children's education, then privileged and high-income groups maintain a permanent advantage over the poorer segments of the population.

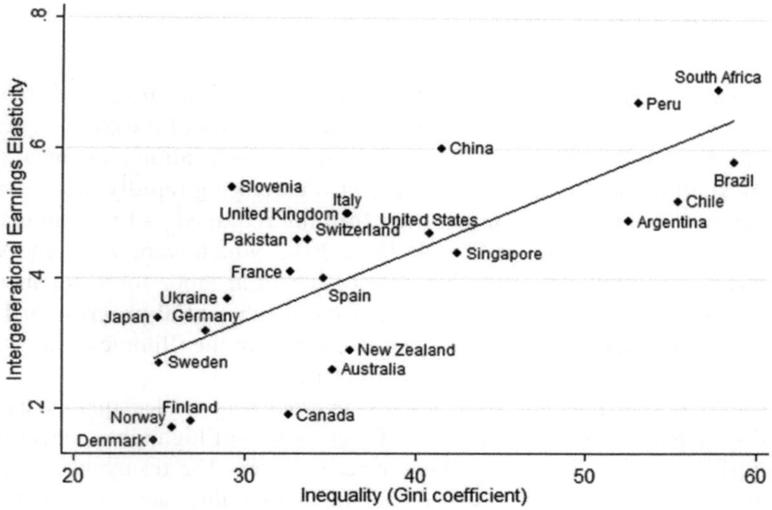

Fig. 6.5 Intergenerational mobility and inequality (*Source*: Corak 2012)

This will in turn reinforce income inequality and inequalities in opportunities and limit intergenerational (or social) mobility.[6]

Despite the lack of official statistics, high social mobility was evident and widely considered one of China's major social achievements before the 1980s. For example, a significant proportion of university students came from poor and rural areas before the 1980s, thanks to the government-supported rural education system and the availability of university scholarships. In recent years, however, this trend has reversed. Figure 6.5 shows that China is now a country of much lower intergenerational earnings mobility and higher income inequality compared with a large pool of countries. The comparison between China and the United States is particularly striking. While income inequality is similar in both countries, the Chinese children from low-income families have much more limited opportunities to climb up the income ladder than their American counterparts.

In contrast, countries, including the Nordic countries, Canada, France, New Zealand, and Australia, that have a tradition of equity-focused public policies, and strong government involvement in the provision of basic social services, see much higher intergenerational mobility (low elasticity) and low income inequality. China's regression in social mobility can be largely attributed to the shrinking role of government in the provision of social services and the increasing importance of private education, while rising income disparities reinforce social inequality and inequality of opportunities.

---

[6] The intergenerational (or social) mobility is commonly measured by intergenerational earnings elasticity—elasticity of earnings between parents and their children (the higher the number, the lower the intergenerational earnings mobility).

6.3 Gender Inequality

It was widely acknowledged that "Chinese women hold up half of the sky," symbolizing the equal role of women in China as a result of progressive gender-focused development. The gender gaps in health and education outcomes, which are almost eliminated in urban areas, are also narrowing rapidly in rural areas. For example, the school enrolment rate for children aged 7–15 in rural China was the same for boys and girls at 98 % in 2010, which were 95 % and 93 %, respectively, in 2000. The illiteracy rate of the rural labor force for men and women was 2.9 % and 12 % in 2002, but more substantial progress had been made for women than men over the past decade, with the illiteracy rate reduced to 2.6 % for men and 9.6 % for women in 2010.

However, despite the impressive progress in promoting gender equality, the 2008 UNDP Millennium Development Goals Progress Report highlights gender equity and equality as a key deficit for China in recent years. The resurgence of gender inequalities is reflected in the excess female infant mortality rate, the gender gap in human capital accumulation, and the unequal employment opportunities.

The excess female infant mortality rate was a result of the deeply rooted son preference in China which manifests in discrimination against girls at birth and deprived access to preventive and curative health care in early childhood (Li et al. 2004). Despite the fact that son preference is often seen as "backward," or a combination of poverty and insularity, sex-selective abortion is actually independent of wealth and income. It is highest, for example, in some of the richest, most open parts of China and India, such as Guangdong province in southern China and Haryana state in north India.

According to the 2012 World Bank report, excess female deaths have risen since 1990 from 890,000 to 1.1 million in 2009. Over a quarter of all excess female deaths in China occur at birth. These are the numbers of "missing girls" if the normal sex ratio at birth of 105 boys to 100 girls had prevailed in China, in contrast to the observed sex ratio of almost 120 boys born for every 100 girls. This problem of "missing girls" was exacerbated in recent decades by the practice of sex-specific abortions (Banister 2004).

Gender disparity in human capital is also on the rise in China in recent years. The human capital indicator measures the level of education attainment, return to schooling and work experience, as well as mandatory retirement age. In China, while the human capital for both females and males increased, the gender disparity also widened. The share of female human capital decreased to 41 % in 2007 from 44 % in 1975, indicating human capital increase was much slower for females than males. Also, female per capita human capital was 13 % lower than male per capita human capital in 1985, but it was 22 % lower in 2007 (Li Haizheng et al. 2009), a result of both lower return to schooling and less working years of females than their male counterparts.

Men and women also face differential employment opportunities. China's labor market is highly segregated by gender. The 2000 census shows that 95 % of females were in low-paid jobs, compared with 90 % of males, despite female average schooling (12 years) being higher than that of males (11 years). Not only were women affected disproportionally by the layoffs of SOE restructuring, they faced also more discrimination in getting subsequent job offers than men did. The mandatory retirement regulations force women to retire at the age of 50 while men can work until the age of 60, depriving women of equal employment opportunities.

In sum while China has made impressive progress in achieving better health and education outcomes compared with countries of similar income levels, recent years saw a rise in social disparity in health and education. The rising inequality in human development indicators can undermine the social mobility that China had successfully achieved in the pre-reform era. If policy measures are not put in place to address social disparities, China will face a self-reinforcing spiral of inequality, with high-income groups capturing disproportionally the gains of China's modernization because they can afford to invest in better education for their children and benefit from the rising demand for skilled job opportunities. On the other hand, disadvantaged groups will be trapped in low-income, low-return economic activities, largely excluded from productive employment opportunities that are made available in the process of production upgrading and economic diversification.

The message from the Chinese experience is clear. By focusing narrowly on the pace of growth, rapid economic expansion may not only fail to bring improvement in well-being, the very goal of economic development, it may even reverse social progress, by eroding human capacities and widening inequality in opportunities. So, economic growth in itself does not guarantee desirable development outcomes, and the role of government is particularly crucial in enhancing individual capabilities in the area of health and education and in promoting equity.

The Chinese government has fully recognized the serious risks associated with rising inequalities and social disparities. In the 12th FYP, promoting inclusive growth to ensure the benefits of economic growth are spread to a greater proportion of Chinese citizens is endorsed as the guiding principle of China's development strategy for the period of 2010–2015. To achieve an inclusive growth and help the disadvantaged population, in recent years, the government policies have focused on improving access to education and health in rural areas while facilitating rural-urban migration. For example, supporting the development of rural boarding schools has been identified as an effective policy that can both improve rural education and encourage rural-urban migration while easing the pressure on social services in urban areas as a result of the large migrant population. In 2011, the central government devoted 47.17 billion yuan (7.9 billion $) to support the 9-year compulsive education for all students in the rural areas, targeting particularly the development of rural boarding schools.

History shows that rising inequity and social disparity is often unavoidable as countries are undergoing major economic transformation, such as the case of China. The role of government, therefore, is critical to mitigate the adverse impact of inequality, maintaining equity as a goal of development. The Chinese government has indeed demonstrated its strong commitment to tackling inequalities through the implementation of a wide range of social policies and programs in recent years. It is the hope of both the Chinese people and the rest of world to see a rising China that is both strong and harmonious, setting an example of successful social and economic transformation for other countries.

References

Banister J (2004) Shortage of girls in China today. J Popul Res 21(1):19–45
Corak M (2012) Inequality from generation to generation: The United States in comparison. In: Rycroft R (ed) The economics of inequality, poverty, and discrimination in the 21st century, ABC-CLIO. Praeger, Santa Barbara
Dollar D (2007) Poverty, inequality and social disparities during China's economic reform. World Bank working paper, Washington, DC
Gu X, Tang S (1995) Reform of the Chinese health care financing system. Health Policy 32:181–191
Haizheng L, Fraumeni BM, Kui ZQ, Wang XJ (2009) Human capital in China, NBER working paper, 15500. National Bureau of Economic Research, Cambridge, MA
Li S, Zhu C, Feldman M (2004) Gender differences in child survival in contemporary rural China: a county study. J Biosoc Sci 36:83–109
Liu Y, Rao K, Fei J (1998) Economic transition and health transition: comparing China and Russia. Health Policy 44:103–122
OECD (2007) OECD environmental performance reviews: China. OECD, Paris
Sen KA (1999) Development as freedom. Oxford University Press, Oxford
Tang SL, Meng QY, Chen L, Bekedam H, Evans T, Whitehead M (2008) Tackling the challenges to health equity in China. Health system reform in China, Published online
UNDP (2005) China human development report. UNDP, Beijing
UNDP (2008) Millenium Development Goals Progress
US Census Bureau Population Division (2005) Interim state population projections. US Census Bureau, Washington, DC

Chapter 7
Daunting Environmental Challenges

China's economic growth miracle in the past few decades has come at a heavy cost. The rapid expansion of production has resulted in severe environmental and resource degradation and excessive greenhouse gas emissions. In addition, the pattern of growth may bring catastrophic consequences for future generations because some of the environmental and resource degradation might be irreversible. This uncertain, but potentially enormous, cost of cleaning up must be borne by future generations who may be deprived of the opportunities to live a safe and clean environment.

China now is facing serious environmental challenges on a massive scale, with severe air and water pollution, heavy metal pollution in the soil, and acute water shortages (SEPA 2010b). The root cause of the escalating environmental crisis is the combination of rapid expansion in energy-intensive, heavy industries with predominantly coal-based energy use that has fueled the GDP growth in the past 10 years. Inadequate policy measures to safeguard the environment and weak enforcement of environment regulations, together with the mind-set of grow first and clean afterward at all levels of governments in China, are all responsible for causing environmental and resource degradation at such a rapid pace.

This chapter examines China's growth from the perspective of environmental and resource sustainability, focusing on the scale of the country's major environmental problems as well as its rapid motorization, rising energy demand, greenhouse gas emissions, and the cost of environmental and resource degradation.

7.1 The Environment and Resource Degradation

7.1.1 A Looming Water Crisis

The World Bank has warned that water scarcity will become an increasingly pressing issue in China (2009). The country's water shortage is a consequence of overuse and declining supplies. From 2000 to 2009, China's total water reserves fell by 1.5 %

X. Wang et al., *The Quality of Growth and Poverty Reduction in China*, International Research on Poverty Reduction, DOI 10.1007/978-3-642-36346-7_7,

annually, about 35 billion cubic meters of water a year according to the Ministry of Water Resources. That is roughly as much water as the Yangtze River pushes past Shanghai in eight months (World Bank 2009).

China has very low water availability per capita and water resources are unevenly distributed across regions. The average water availability is only about 1,850 m^3 per capita, less than one quarter of the world average. The water shortages are particularly acute in the north where half of the population lives with only 15 % of China's total water resources. Among the 600 larger cities, 400 suffer from water shortages according to the 2007 OECD Environmental Performance Reviews of China.

The deterioration of water quality caused by widespread pollution further aggravates water shortages in China. According to the OECD report, about 30 % of the rivers monitored are classified as worse than grade V (i.e., highly polluted), three quarters of China's major lakes are also considered to be highly polluted (grade V or above), and a quarter of China's coastal waters are very polluted (grade IV or above).

Water pollution in China is caused primarily by chemical fertilizers and pesticides, industrial waste, and raw sewage. China's first pollution census published in 2010 revealed fertilizer use was a bigger source of water contamination than factory effluent. China's intensity of use of both chemical fertilizers and pesticides is three to four times higher than the OECD average.[1]

Factor reallocation and poor selection of plant locations have exacerbated water contamination in China. In 2006, as many as 81 % of the total 7,555 chemical and petrochemical construction projects were located in environmentally sensitive areas, such as rivers, lakes, and densely populated areas, while 45 % of those were high-risk pollution sources (SEPA 2010a).

7.1.2 *Worst Air Quality in the World*

Air quality in China's cities is the worst in the world (Zhang et al. 2010). When viewed from space, wrote space shuttle astronaut Jay Apt in National Geographic, "many of the great coastal cities of China hide from our cameras under a blanket of smoke from soft-coal fires." For example, the northeast industrial town of Benxi is so polluted that it once disappeared from satellite photos, and its residents have the highest rate of lung disease in China. According to official statistics, in 2013 concentrations of PM2.5—the tiny airborne particles considered most harmful to health—were more than 30 times the World Health Organization's recommended standard in many cities in 2013.

A World Bank study shows that 16 Chinese cities are among the world's 20 most polluted cities, and only 1 % of the China's 560 million city dwellers breathe air

[1] About 11.7 million pounds of organic pollutants are emitted into Chinese waters every day, compared to 5.5 in the United States, 3.4 in Japan, 2.3 in Germany, 3.2 in India, and 0.6 in South Africa.

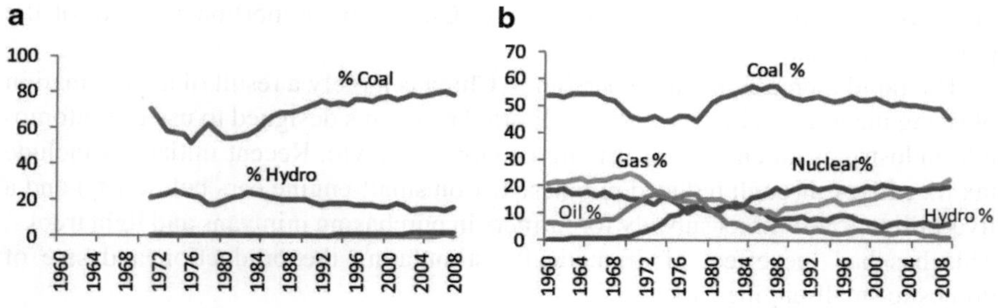

Fig. 7.1 Energy source of electricity production: (**a**) China and (**b**) United States (*Source*: Authors' construction based on the World Bank database)

considered safe by European Union standards. About a third of 113 cities surveyed failed to meet national air quality standards in 2009 based on Chinese official data (air pollution levels set by China's national air quality standards are 4–5 times higher than OECD standards).

The main sources of outdoor air pollution in China are coal combustion, motor vehicle exhaust, and the massive scale of urban construction, generating particles of soot, organic hazardous material, heavy metals, acid aerosols, and dust, in addition to emissions of sulfur dioxide (SO_2) and nitrogen dioxide (NO_2). The particulate matter that is less than 10 μm (PM10) poses the biggest health threat. In China, PM10 accounts for about 72 %, SO_2 8 %, and NO_2 0.3 % of primary pollutants of concern between 2000 and 2007 (Andrews 2011).

Coal, the number one source of air pollution in China, is also the principal source of energy. Figure 7.1 shows that about 80 % of electricity and 70 % of total energy in China were produced from coal (much of it polluting high-sulfur coal), compared with only 45 % in the United States. The rapid growth of private car ownership in recent years has escalated air pollution problems in urban areas.

7.2 Rapid Motorization

As the fastest-growing economy in the world, China is experiencing a rapid increase in motor vehicle ownership. Between 2002 and 2007, China's national automobile market grew by an average of 21 %, or one million new vehicles year-on-year. In 2009, 13.759 million motor vehicles were manufactured in China, surpassing the United States as the world's largest automobile producer by volume (Yu Hong and Yang Mu 2010). China has by far the highest growth rate of vehicle ownership, 10.6 % annually, followed by India (7 %) and Indonesia (6.5 %). China's rapid expansion in car ownership has important implications for transport, urban infrastructure, and environment. Furthermore, it affects oil demand and, by extension, the stability of the world oil market due to China's disproportionate share of the global oil demand.[2]

The rapid increase of car ownership in China is largely a result of a combination of rising incomes and government-supported programs designed to use the automobile industry as an engine for driving economic growth. Recent initiatives include tax incentives through reduced purchase tax on small-engine cars below 1.6 l and a five-billion RMB direct subsidy for farmers in purchasing minivans and light trucks. This has had the effect of dramatically stimulating the production and sale of domestic small-engine cars.

The environmental cost of rapid motorization in China, which has been largely overlooked during the expansion of the automobile industry in the past decade, is escalating. Rapid motorization in cities has led to rising congestion levels, increased air pollution, increased oil consumption, and a high traffic fatality rate. According to a 2010 study by IMB of 20 large cities, Beijing and Mexico City have the worst traffic in the world. Too many cars on the roads are bringing cities to a standstill in China. Urban congestion was one of the serious issues discussed at the annual sessions of the National People's Congress and the Chinese People's Political Consultative Conference National Committee in 2011. Unfortunately, to date, no studies have fully investigated the total economic costs of congestion, in terms of time lost and productivity.

Trends of private car use and oil demand place enormous strains on urban infrastructure and energy imports. The constraints imposed by very high population densities and the limited amount of land available for residential and commercial development, as well as strict protections on agricultural land around cities, show that Chinese cities cannot physically expand as rapidly as motorization increases. However, the policy incentives designed to stimulate economic growth through a rapid increase in private car ownership have led many city governments to respond to motor vehicle congestion by expanding existing lanes and building more roads. Despite this expansion to make room for cars, congestion levels have spiraled upward and average travel speeds downward. A study of six large Chinese cities from 2000 to 2006 shows that although the amount of road space per capita has increased in major Chinese cities, road space per private car has dropped significantly (Table 7.1). In comparison, London, Tokyo, and New York City had more road length and road length per capita than all Chinese cities.

Emissions from vehicles make up a high and rising proportion of total urban air pollution, and this phenomenon is increasingly being observed in many Chinese cities, as air pollution from industry and households is gradually declining.

[2]Dargay et al. project the total vehicle stock for 45 countries based on the model that factors in key country characteristics such as urbanization, population density, and economic growth. While the global total vehicle stock will increase from about 800 million in 2002 to over 2 billion units in 2030, China's vehicle stock will increase nearly 20-fold, to 390 million in 2030. By 2030, the six countries with the largest number of vehicles, ranked in descending order, will be China, United States, India, Japan, Brazil, and Mexico.

Table 7.1 Private cars and road space in Chinese cities: 2000 and 2006

City	Year	Private car (million)	Road length (km)	Paved road (m^2 per cap)	Road space (m^2 per car)
Beijing	2000	0.49	3,624	3.7	85
	2006	1.81	5,866	7.4	54
Tianjin	2000	0.21	3,608	6.1	200
	2006	0.55	5,991	13.8	145
Shanghai	2000	0.05	6,641	7.2	1,607
	2006	0.51	14,619	11.8	422
Chongqing	2000	0.06	2,693	2.4	438
	2006	0.28	4,011	8.1	243
Guangzhou	2000	0.22	2,053	8.2	125
	2006	0.62	5,208	13.9	140
Xi'an	2000	0.07	975	5.14	134
	2006	0.26	1,480	8.6	125
Average	2000	–	–	5.5	431
	2006	–	–	10.6	188

Studies have shown that 45–60 % of NOx emissions and 85 % of CO emissions are from mobile sources in most Chinese cities. It is estimated that by 2010 in Shanghai, vehicular emissions will produce 75 % of total NOx emissions, 94 % of total CO emissions, and 98 % of total hydrocarbon (HC) emissions. Even with stricter emissions controls and cleaner fuels, mobile-source pollution is likely to continue rising due to increased use of individual vehicles and longer trip lengths. Because of the high physical density of both people and motor vehicles in Chinese cities, public exposure to direct inhalation of vehicle emissions is high. The scarcity of space simply makes the impact of emissions from vehicles more dangerous to pedestrians. Respiratory diseases, such as infections, asthma, and decreased lung efficiency, are common in polluted urban areas.

In March 2009, the government released a new development outline for the automobile industry from 2009 to 2011 (see Appendix 3). The new policy framework maps out comprehensive development schemes, such as industrial upgrading, technological enhancement, and promotion of new engines, and addresses other issues such as the lack of economy of scale and production fragmentation. The policy support to the development of vehicles using renewable energy represents major progress in addressing issues of environment and greenhouse gas emissions (see Appendix 4). However, the promotion of environment-friendly vehicles in China has lagged behind that of other advanced nations. The development of green-energy technology is a major challenge for the Chinese automobile industry, and the environmental benefits are unlikely to be realized in many years to come unless policy measures can be enforced to moderate the growth of private car ownership.

7.3 Energy Demand and Greenhouse Gas Emissions

7.3.1 Intensive Energy Use

Along with China's structural transformation and rapid growth, the energy use and energy intensity (measured by energy use per unit of GDP) have also evolved over time. China experienced rapid improvement in energy efficiency from 1978 to 2000; on average the energy use of one unit of GDP is eight times less today than in 1980 (Fig. 6.2). The improvement in energy efficiency stems from development policies that focused on production upgrading and fostering economic sectors in line with China's comparative advantages, i.e., abundant laborers, relatively scarce natural resources and raw materials, and a lower level of capital stock.

As discussed in the previous chapters, China's growth pattern prior to 2000 was characterized by labor-intensive light manufacturing. However, the trend in energy efficiency improvement reversed in the early 2000s (Fig. 7.2). Between 2000 and 2008, total energy consumption increased twofold, with energy import rising from 1 % of total energy consumption in 1990 to 13 % in 2008 (see Table 7.2). The growth of energy consumption outpaced GDP growth, with energy demand elasticity (the ratio of energy demand growth to GDP growth) increased from less than 0.5 between 1978 and 2000 to 1.5 between 2000 and 2006 (Rosen and Houser 2007) (Fig. 7.3).

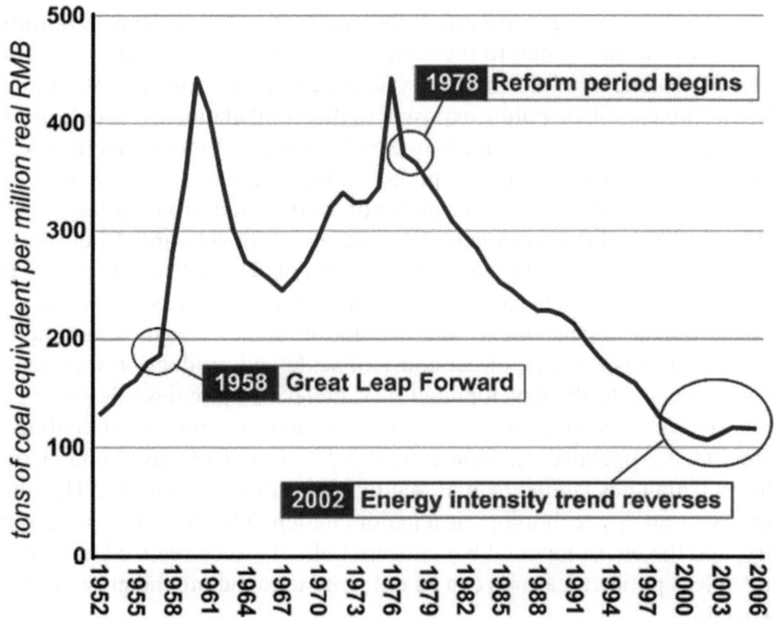

Fig. 7.2 *Source*: IEA, World Energy Outlook (2006)

Table 7.2 China's overall energy balance sheet (10,000 tons of SCE)

	1990	1995	2000	2005	2008
Energy dependency					
Total energy available for consumption	96,138	129,535	142,605	232,225	287,011
Total energy consumption	98,703	131,176	145,531	235,997	291,448
Imports	1,310	5,456	14,334	26,952	36,764
(Import as % energy use)	1	4	10	11	13
Energy use by sector					
Industry	67,578	96,191	103,774	168,724	209,302
(As % energy use)	68	73	71	71	72
Construction	1,213	1,335	2,179	3,403	3,813
(As % energy use)	1	1	1	1	1
Transport, storage, and post	4,541	5,863	11,242	18,391	22,917
(As % energy use)	5	4	8	8	8
Household consumption	15,799	15,745	15,614	25,305	31,898
(As % energy use)	16	12	11	11	11

Source: Authors' construction based on China Statistical Yearbooks

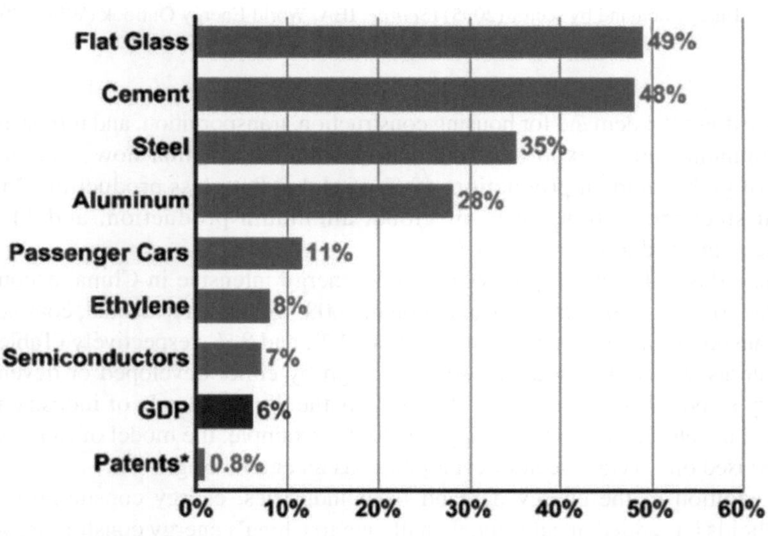

Fig. 7.3 China's share of global production (2006) (*Source*: IEA, World Energy Outlook (WEO) 2006)

Since 2000, China has embarked on a growth path that is dominated by energy-intensive industries, relying on scarce resources including water and raw materials, while creating relatively fewer jobs. These industries produced energy-intensive products, such as steel, aluminum, and cement, to meet China's

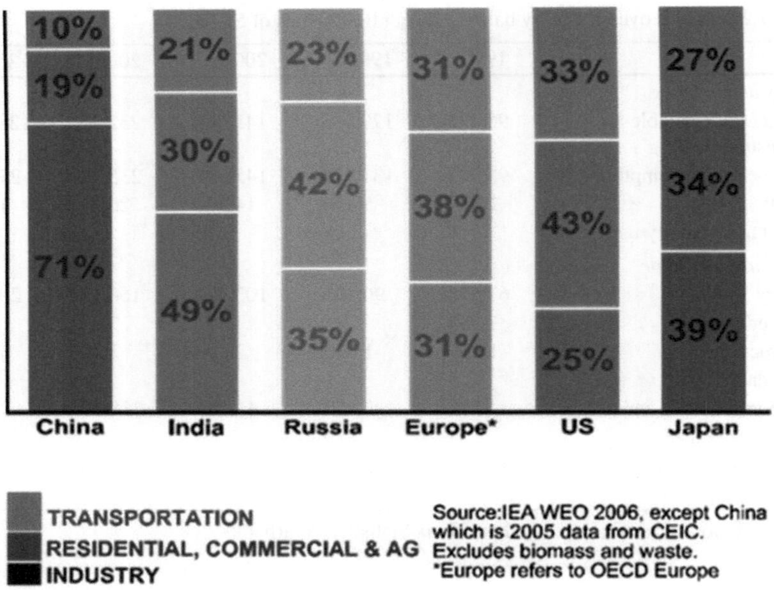

Fig. 7.4 Energy demand by sector (2005) (*Source*: IEA, World Energy Outlook (WEO) 2006)

massive domestic demand for housing construction, transportation, and infrastructure development and to export to international markets. China now accounts for 48 % of global cement production, 49 % of global flat glass production, 35 % of global steel production, 28 % of global aluminum production, and 11 % of passage car productions (Fig. 6.3).

The industrial sector is overwhelmingly energy intensive in China, accounting for over 70 % of final energy consumption in 2008, while the residential, commercial, and transportation sectors account for 11 %, 2 %, and 8 %, respectively (Table 7.2). The energy use in the industrial sector is high by either developed or developing country standards (see Fig. 7.4). This reflects the dominant role of industry in the Chinese development model, as opposed to, for example, the model of India, which has focused on services sector development as an engine of growth.

In addition to the energy demand from industries, energy consumption from households has added an additional challenge to China's energy constraints. Within less than a decade, energy consumption from households increased over twofold, from 157,990 thousand tons of SEC in 2000 to 318,980 in 2008 (see Table 7.2). In 2008, the share of the country's energy demand from consumers in the form of heating, cooling, lighting, and transportation accounted for about 11 % of total energy use. China now ranks with middle-income countries, and energy-intensive consumer goods, like air conditioners and automobiles, are within reach of many Chinese

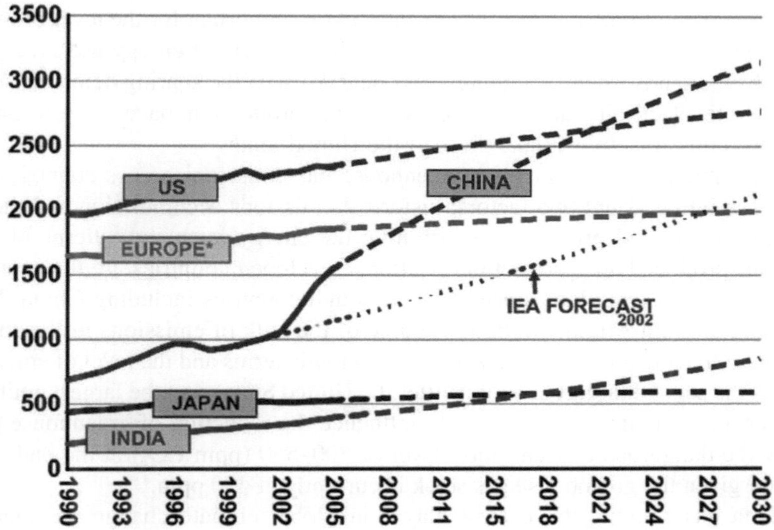

Fig. 7.5 *Source*: IEA WEO (2002), IEA WEO (2006). Excludes biomass and wastes (*Europe refers to OECD Europe)

households, as reflected in the rapid increase of private car ownership. The continuous fast economic growth will be adding an increasing pressure on energy demand, posing major challenges in meeting its 12th FYP energy intensity reduction target of 16 % between 2010 and 2015 (Howes 2010) (Fig. 7.5).

Clearly, China is on a development path that features unsustainable production and consumption patterns. Based on current energy consumption, the IEA has raised their China 2030 forecast by 1.2 billion tons of oil equivalent, a 63 % upward revision (IEA 2006; see Fig. 6.5). Under this scenario, China will account for 20 % of global energy demand, more than Europe and Japan combined, and easily surpass the United States as the world's largest energy consumer within the next decade.

7.3.2 The Largest Greenhouse Emitter in the World

In 2007, China surpassed the United States to become the largest greenhouse gas emitter. China produced 6,200 metric tons of CO_2 in 2007, compared with 5,800 metric tons from the United States, although China's CO_2 emission per capita remains relatively low—about a quarter of that in the United States and half that of the United Kingdom.[3] Two factors are particularly important for the level of overall emissions: rising energy intensity and the carbon content of energy use. According to the Netherlands Environmental Assessment Agency, the soaring demand for coal to generate electricity and a surge in cement production have caused China's recorded emissions to overtake those of the United States.

In ascribing responsibility for greenhouse gas emissions across countries, one must take into account two factors: historical emissions accumulation and the fact that consumers and producers determining the energy intensity patterns of commodities produced and production location. Developed countries are the source of around 70 % of emissions since 1950, although countries including China, India, Brazil, and South Africa will be the source of the bulk of emissions in the coming decades. Given China's enormity both in economic terms and the level of emissions (i.e., as the second largest economy after the United States and the largest emitter in the world), the country, by itself, can influence the reduction of greenhouse gases below the dangerous concentration level of 500–550 (ppm CO_2) at the end of the century given the greenhouse gas stock is currently at 430 ppm.[4]

China has become the central player in global climate change negotiations. However, contrary to suggestions by some that China does not take climate change seriously, in recent years, the government has devoted enormous resources to reduce energy use and emissions and to improve energy efficiency. In the 12th Five-Year Plan, the Chinese government set a range of targets to reduce CO_2 emissions. These include reducing energy consumption per unit of gross domestic product (GDP) by 20 % by 2010, increasing the share of renewable energy to about 10 % of total energy use, as well as covering roughly 20 % of the nation's land with forest by 2020.

However, climate change is an issue of global environmental problems which requires actions both at the national and international levels. In particular, the linkages between trade and climate change are particularly critical. The recent World Bank study (2008) shows that while in addressing climate change, it is critical to

---

[3] The figures are estimated by the Netherlands Environmental Assessment Agency. They only include carbon dioxide emissions from fossil fuel burning and cement production. They do not include sources of other greenhouse gases, such as methane from agriculture and nitrous oxide from industrial processes. And they exclude other sources of carbon dioxide, such as from the aviation and shipping industries, as well as from deforestation, gas flaring, and underground coal fires.

The primary data sources are from the oil company BP on the consumption of oil, gas, and coal across the world during 2006, as well as information on cement production published by the US Geological Survey. Cement production, which requires huge amounts of energy, accounts for about 4 % of global CO_2 production from fuel use and industrial sources. China's cement industry, which has rapidly expanded in recent years and now produces about 44 % of world supply, contributes almost 9 % of the country's CO_2 emissions. The carbon dioxide emissions are calculated from each country's use of oil, gas, and coal using UN conversion factors.

[4] It is widely accepted that temperature increase more than 2 °C would be dangerous, therefore the limiting greenhouse gas concentration at a level that leads to 2 °C increase with small probability is set as an emission reduction goal. The estimates from the Hadley Centre models show that the concentration levels (ppm CO_2e) associated with the probabilities of 2–3 °C temperature increase are 450 (78 %), 500 (96 %), 550 (99 %), and 650 (100 %). Given the current level of 430 ppm, we have probably missed the chance of keeping emission below 450 ppm by the end of century.

ensure commitment and participation of developing countries, in particular China and India, the current tariffs and nontariff barriers are major impediments to the diffusion of clean energy technology in developing countries. International collaborations in policies that facilitate the trade between developing countries (South-South trade) in promoting clean energy technology are likely to bring huge benefits both in reducing emissions and economic and social benefits.

7.4 The Cost of Environmental and Resource Degradation

As China progresses to become a middle-income country, thanks to fast growth, the environmental challenges and severe degradation of natural resources and ecosystem are posing a serious health risk to its population and a potential threat to its future growth.

7.4.1 Health Cost

Environmental risk factors, in particular, air, water, and industrial waste-related pollution, are a major source of morbidity and mortality in China. Despite the frequent references to China's environmental risks in global policy discussion, comprehensive analyses of environmental indicators and health outcomes through scientific publications and popular media are absent (Zhang et al. 2010). The scarcity of systematically collected data for monitoring and evaluating environmental risks in China is partially responsible for the lack of systematic empirical studies. On the other hand, reliable data for industrial emissions are rarely made available to the public. For example, national assessments of drinking water quality are seldom taken, with the last one conducted in 1998.

Based on Chinese official data, a majority (about 75 %) of the water flowing through urban areas is unsuitable for drinking or fishing, and over 300 million people living in rural areas have no access to safe drinking water. The economic cost of disease and premature deaths associated with the incidence of diarrhea and cancer in rural China is about 0.49 % of GDP (World Bank 2008). Recent studies suggest that drinking water contamination is a major factor for digestive system cancers, including stomach, liver, esophageal, and colorectal cancers. These cancers have the highest mortality rate of malignant neoplasms in China at 73 per 100,000 cases in 2005 (China Health Yearbooks).

Studies also show that outdoor air pollution is associated with a significant health cost. Based on existing evidence, outdoor air pollution in China is associated with about 300,000 deaths, 20 million cases of respiratory illnesses, and 5.5 million cases of chronic bronchitis each year. The overall cost of health damage is estimated to be between 1.8 and 4.7 % of GDP (World Bank 2007; Millman et al. 2008) and projected to reach 13 % of GDP by 2020 (Ho 2006).

The Chinese population is also subject to heavy metal pollution in the soil. It is estimated that about 70 % of electronic waste generated worldwide is processed in China, which poses substantial risks to human health and the environment (Ni and Zeng 2009). The energy-intensive manufacturing activities that have been driving China's economic growth in the past few decades generate pollution from heavy metals such as lead, mercury, chromium, cadmium, and arsenic, which have become increasingly prevalent in China and pose a serious health risk to the population. However, data scarcity has limited a full investigation of the health cost of industrial waste-related pollution.

Evidently, the quality of life of the Chinese population is at a stake when the quality of growth is disregarded by the blind pursuit of the pace of growth. In light of data limitations and our insufficient understanding of the potential transmission channels from environmental risks to health outcomes, the true scale of the health cost of pollution from various sources in China is yet to be unveiled. The estimated health cost reported from existing studies that are based on data sources from various parts of China is likely to underestimate the impact on health for the whole population.

7.4.2 The Choking Point

The rising resource scarcity and degradation will not only pose a significant health risk to the Chinese population today and in many years to come but can also act as a constraint on future economic growth. The increasingly fierce competition between energy and water has brought China to the choking point, limiting the country's future development prospect. Agriculture and the coal industry are China's two largest water users. In 2010, the agricultural and coal sectors together used about 85 % of the 599 billion cubic meters (158 trillion gallons) of water resources.

Water scarcity has become a limiting factor in sustaining the scale of China's agricultural production. In northern China, water shortages have also forced farmers to use wastewater for the irrigation of about 40,000 km^2 of agricultural land, resulting in the contamination of food by heavy metals. This provides another channel of exposure to water pollution, transferring water pollution to soil pollution (Zhang et al. 2010). Although the prevalence of such incidence across China is largely unknown due to lack of monitoring data and a fully functioning surveillance system, the reality of water shortages is likely to lead to increased usage of unsafe water for food production and processing.

Water scarcity is also limiting the capacity of natural bodies of water to serve their ecological functions. The excessive surface water withdrawals have made it impossible to sustain a minimum level of environmental and ecological flows for major rivers in northern China. Water shortages have also led to overexploitation of groundwater, and consequently, the lowering of water tables, drying up of lakes and wetlands, and land subsidence are frequent occurrences in many cities (World Bank 2008).

China's desire to reduce carbon emissions through clean coal use and development of hydropower is seriously constrained by water shortages. Even as China is expanding low water-intensive energy sources, such as solar, wind, hydro, and nuclear power development, coal-based energy demand is still increasing rapidly. China's coal mining, processing, combustion, and coal-to-chemical industries consume more water than any other industrial, municipal, or commercial sector. Hydropower development increases water scarcity. Already the largest producer of hydropower in the world, China's plan to triple hydropower capacity by 2020 is likely to be constrained by water availability.

The costs of cleaning up can also act as a limit on China's future growth. In addition to the cost of cleaning up contaminated water, land, and air, pollution is costing China billions in additional health costs, lost productivity, and early mortality. According to World Bank estimates, China's environmental costs come to around $100 billion a year, or about 5.8 % of GDP, including the impact on mortality.

7.5 Responding to Environmental Challenges

The Chinese government has responded proactively to the serious environmental challenges on several fronts. First, it has been working with great determination in recent years to develop a comprehensive framework of environmental laws and regulations. Second, it has focused on how this legislation can be effectively implemented and enforced. To this end, a major effort has been made to clarify the roles of the national and provincial governments and to strengthen the operation of the legal system. Third, it has significantly improved access to government-held environmental information with the introduction of the environmental information disclosure policy in 2008. A substantial amount of environmental information has been disclosed by environmental agencies at all levels of governments. In some cities, local environmental protection bureaus (EPB) have set up online mechanisms to facilitate access to environmental information and the submission of information requests by the public.

China's 11th and 12th Five-Year Plans (FYP) have incorporated binding environmental targets into national development policy (see Table 7.3). During the period of the 11th FYP (2005–2010), important progress was made in several areas: the chemical oxygen and sulfur dioxide emissions were decreased by 12.45 % and 14.29 %, respectively, exceeding the emission reduction targets; the capacity of water pollution control facilities in major cities increased from 52 % in 2005 to 72 % in 2010; the control sections of surface water quality that were classed as grade III (good) increased to 51.9 %; and the average concentration of sulfur dioxide in urban areas decreased by 26.3 % (China Ministry of Environment website, http://zfs.mep.gov.cn).

Despite this progress, the overall trend of environmental deterioration in China has not yet been halted, highlighting the urgent need to continue efforts from all levels of government and the private sector, including enterprises, farmers, and

Table 7.3 Environmental and resources targets

Target	11th FYP 2010 Target	11th FYP 2010 Actual	12th FYP 2010	12th FYP 2015	% reduction
Reduction in energy intensity per unit of GDP	20 %	19.10 %			16 %
Reduction in water consumption per unit of industrial value added	30 %	36.70 %			30 %
% of control sections of surface water quality worse than grade V			17.7	<15	2.70 %
% of control sections of water quality among seven major water systems better than grade III			55	>60	5 %
Increase of water efficiency coefficient in agriculture	0.5	0.5			0.53
Farmland reserves (million hectares)	120	121.2			121.2
Forest coverage	20 %	20.36 %			21.66 %
Forest stock (trillion cubic meters)	N/A	13.7			14.3
Reduction in carbon emissions per unit of GDP	N/A	N/A			17 %
Non-fossil fuel as % of primary energy	N/A	8.30 %			11.40 %
Reduction in emissions of major pollutions					
Reduction in chemical oxygen demand (COD) (10,000 tons)	N/A	N/A	2,551.7	2,347.6	8 %
Reduction in sulfur dioxide (10,000 tons)	N/A	N/A	2,267.8	2,086.4	8 %
Reduction in ammonia nitrogen (10,000 tons)	N/A	N/A	264.4	238	10 %
Reduction in nitrous oxides (10,000 tons)	N/A	N/A	2,273.6	2,046.2	10 %

consumers. The 12th FYP marks a major policy shift from the past growth-centered development strategy to the creation of a society that balances economic growth with resource conservation and environmental protection.

In the 12th FYP (2011–2015), the Chinese government places high priority both on climate change and environmental issues—conserving energy and cleaning up the environment are among the five key goals set for the next 5 years (in addition to encouraging domestic consumption, developing the services sector, and moving to higher value-added manufacturing). Binding targets for a range of environmental and energy issues, including important air and water quality pollutants, are included for the first time in the national Five-Year Plan.

In addition, several major environmental protection programs have also been proposed to address pollution issues as well as energy and ecological resources conservation in the 12th FYP. The programs for pollution control include (1) water pollution control in major river basins, (2) smoke desulfurization in coal-fired power plants, (3) disposal of medical waste and hazardous waste, (4) the nuclear and radiation safety program, and (5) chromium slag pollution control.

The energy programs (see Box 7.1) are designed to promote a pattern of economic growth based on the principle of "reducing, reusing, and recycling." In the area of ecological conservation and restoration (see Box 7.2), the policy focus has shifted from posttreatment to prevention, and from artificial improvement to natural restoration, aiming to reverse the trend of ecological deterioration at the source.

Another important policy development in the 12th FYP is the goal set for developing a circular economy (CE) as illustrated in Fig. 7.6. The concept of CE has

Box 7.1: Priority Programs of Energy Conservation

Upgrading of Low-Efficiency Coal-Fired Industrial Boiler
District Heat and Power Cogeneration
Recovery of Residual Heat and Pressure
Oil Saving and Substitution
Energy Conservation of Motor System
Optimization of Energy System
Energy Conservation in Buildings
Green Lighting
Energy Conservation in Government Agencies
Building the Energy Conservation Monitoring and Technological Support System

Source: 12th Five-Year Plan

Box 7.2: Priority Programs of Ecological Conservation

Conservation of Natural Forest Resources
Converting Cultivated Land Back to Forest or Grassland
Converting Grazing Land Back to Grassland
Beijing-Tianjin Sandstorm Source Control
The Shelter Forest System
Wetland Conservation and Restoration
Ecological Conservation and Improvement of the Three-River Headwaters Natural Reserve in Qinghai Province
The Soil and Water Conservation Program
Wild Life Protection and the Construction of Natural Reserves
Integrated Combating Measures for Litho-Desertification

Source: 12th Five-Year Plan

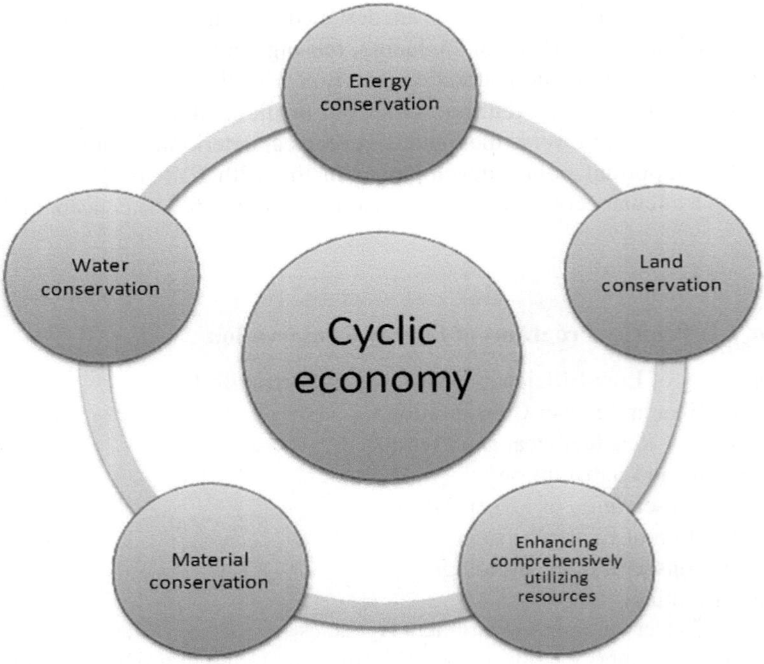

Fig. 7.6 China's circular economy plan (2011–2015) (*Source*: Authors' construction based on the Outline of 12th Five-Year Plan)

three basic principles: recycle, reuse, and reduce. Based on the definition developed by China's National Development and Reform Commission (NDRC), CE has the following key elements:

> CE may be interlinked manufacturing and service businesses seeking the enhancement of economy and environmental performance through collaboration in managing environmental and resource issues. The theme of the CE concept is the exchange of materials where one facility's waste – including energy, water, materials and information – is another facility's input. By working together, the community of businesses seeks a collective benefit that is larger than the sum of the individual benefits each enterprise, industry and community would realize if it intended to optimize its performance on an individual basis (i.e. industrial symbiosis).

In 2010, the Chinese government doubled its investment in developing a circular economy to 2 billion yuan ($300 million) to support the national policies of energy conservation and emission reduction (NDRC 2010). The investment for the 12th FYP period will be used mainly in replacing obsolete production capacity and controlling energy-intensive and polluting industries.

The environmental challenges that China faces are indeed enormous. They are compounded by the country's high population density and the urgent need to lift a large number of people out of poverty through sustained and fast economic growth.

However, the strong commitment from the government to protect the environment and ecosystem and conserve national resources, as reflected in the 12th FYP and in efforts to enforce comprehensive environmental regulations, provides a basis for being optimistic about China's development over the coming decades.

Indeed, China has become the largest investor in clean energy technology—its investment of $34.6 billion accounted for about 21 % of global total investment in clean energy in 2008. In 2009, China overtook the United States to become the leading producer in renewable energy technologies. All of this inspires confidence that China will be able to further its economic transformation and production upgrading, embarking on a development path that is sustainable and low carbon.

References

Andrews SQ (2011) Beijing's hazardous blue sky. http://www.chinadialogue.net/

Ho P (2006) Trajectories for greening in China: between theory and practice. Dev Change 37(1):3–28

Howes S (2010) China's energy intensity target: on-track or off? East Asia Forum, 31 March Canberra, ANU. http://www.eastasiaforum.org/2010/03/31/chinas-energy-intensity-target-on-track-or-off/

IEA (2002) World energy outlook 2002. International Energy Agency, Paris

IEA (2006) World energy outlook 2002. International Energy Agency, Paris

Millman A, Tang D, Perera FP (2008) Air pollution threatens the health of children in China. Pediatrics 122(3):620–628

National Research Council (2005) Urbanization, energy, and air pollution in China: the challenges ahead – proceedings of a symposium. The National Academies Press, Washington, DC

Ni HG, Zeng EY (2009) Law enforcement and global collaboration are the keys to containing e-waste tsunami in China. Environ Sci Technol 43(11):3991–3994

OECD (2007) OECD environmental performance reviews: China. OECD, Paris

Rosen DH, Houser T (2007) China energy: a guide for the perplexed. China balance sheet – a joint project by the Center for Strategic and International Studies and the Peterson Institute for International Economics, Washington, DC

SEPA (2010a) Environmental risk survey of the chemical and petrochemical project in China. http://env.people.com.cn

SEPA (2010b) State of the environment report. State Environmental Protection Administration, Beijing, 2006

World Bank (2007) Cost of Pollution in China: Economic Estimates of Physical Damages. World Bank, Washington, DC. Available: http://siteresources.worldbank.org/INTEAPREGTOP ENVIRONMENT/Resources/China_Cost_of_Pollution.pdf. Accessed on Dec 2012

World Bank (2008) International trade and climate change: economic, legal and institutional perspective. World Bank, Washington, DC

World Bank (2009) Addressing China's water scarcity: recommendations for selected water resource management issues. World Bank, Washington, DC

Yu Hong, Yang Mu (2010) China's automobile industry: an update. EAI background brief no. 500. National University of Singapore, Singapore

Zhang J, Denise L, Mauzerall Z, Tong L, Ezzati M, Remais JV (2010) Environmental health in China: progress towards clean air and safe water. Lancet 375:1110–1119

Conclusions

The global growth experience, including the China case study presented in this book, reaffirms that it is the quality of growth, with its emphasis on growth rate, poverty reduction, equity, and environmental and resource sustainability, not the pace of growth, that can advance development and improve well-being. China's three decades of economic development between 1978 and 2010 show that economic growth can be a powerful force for lifting people out of poverty. However, growth in itself does not guarantee the achievement of desirable development outcomes as measured by improvements in health and education, equity, and equality of opportunities—neither does it ensure environmental and resource sustainability. The role of government is critical in key areas, particularly in those where markets fail to function effectively, such as in human capital accumulation, in natural capital conservation, and in the mitigation of negative production externalities (e.g., oversupply of pollution and excessive carbon emissions leading to global climate change).

Before China's economic growth took off in the early 1970s and 1980s, the government's proactive social policies and investment in social services provision led to an increase in life expectancy to about 67, which was higher than many middle-income countries. But as China's economic status elevated to the ranks of middle-income countries in recent years, its health outcomes became stagnant, while social disparities in health and education, both in terms of access and outcomes, widened. The impressive achievements in gender equality before the early 1980s have even reversed in recent years, as reflected in excess female infant mortality and in a widening gender gap in human capital accumulation and employment opportunities. This trend of social inequity in China has been highlighted in the 2008 UNDP Millennium Development Goals Progress Report.

In achieving equity, history shows that public policies, rather than market forces, are the most important sources of assurance. This is particularly true when countries are undergoing major economic transformation and fast growth, as these processes are often accompanied by rising income inequality. The case of China reinforces this conclusion. While China achieved a record growth rate for over

X. Wang et al., *The Quality of Growth and Poverty Reduction in China*,
International Research on Poverty Reduction, DOI 10.1007/978-3-642-36346-7,

three decades, it has also transformed from an egalitarian society into one with a highly unequal income distribution, at a level approaching that of many Latin American countries, historically the most unequal in the world.

Unlike the situation in many countries burdened with large budget deficits and slow growth, the fiscal capacity of the Chinese government increased by over 22 times between 1980 and 2010. However, the role of government in social services provision is shrinking, and the share of government social spending is significantly lower than that in developed economies despite China's strong fiscal capacity. In many respects, rapid economic growth and the erosion of the role of government in social development have heightened the population's insecurity and income inequality as well as reinforced disparities in human capital accumulation and equality of opportunities.

If public policies are not urgently put in place to address these trends, China is in danger of embarking on a course of a self-reinforcing spiral of inequality. While high-income groups continue to invest in the human capital of their children and benefit from the rising returns to education and skills, disadvantaged groups will be trapped in low-income, low-return economic activities and excluded from China's ongoing growth process. The rising income inequality in China can also become a major source of social and political instability, posing a grave risk to future growth and development.

China has indeed created an economic growth miracle, sustaining high GDP growth over three decades, at a rate unmatched by any other country in history. The economic growth success in the first two decades, in the 1980s and 1990s, stemmed mainly from China's far-reaching reforms of its economic system and its "open-door" policies. In contrast to many transitional and emerging economies which also implemented similar reform policies, the pragmatic implementation of the reform programs and gradual introduction of a range of liberalization policies ensured rapid economic growth while maintaining macroeconomic and political stability. China's success in the smooth transition was largely attributable to the stewardship of a strong and credible government that was committed to transforming the nation from one of the poorest countries in the world to a prosperous and harmonious society.

China's first two decades of growth are marked by the transformation from an agriculture-based economy to one dominated by industry and services sectors and by the elevation of the country to middle-income status. Economic growth in the first two decades was largely driven by productivity growth, resulting from more efficient resource allocation as the centrally planned system was replaced by a more market-oriented economy. The rapid productivity growth in the agricultural sector, a result of introducing the household responsibility and land contract system, together with price liberalization, made it possible for the release of rural surplus of labor to facilitate the rapid expansion of industrial and services sectors and the process of urbanization.

Production and technology upgrading also took place at a fast pace through the restructuring of SOEs and technology transfer brought by FDI and the operation of special economic zones. Integration into the world economy through trade and FDI also played an important role in China's sustained growth; with access to international export markets, China was able to explore its comparative advantages in low-cost labor and economies of scale, improving efficiency and productivity. The inclusive pattern of growth in the 1980s and 1990s was instrumental in expanding employment opportunities for the majority of the Chinese population and lifting over 500 million people out of extreme poverty.

This past decade, between 2000 and 2010, however, China's economic growth was driven largely by excessive capital accumulation and growth in energy-intensive industries, such as automobiles, steel, and cement. This growth pattern was associated with structural imbalances and unprecedented growth in fixed-asset investment, while domestic consumption failed to keep up. The national income distribution skewed toward enterprises in the form of profits and government in the form of tax income, while the share of household income in the national economy eroded to an exceedingly low level by international standards. The sectoral imbalances were more striking, with an over-dominating industrial sector and a significantly underdeveloped services sector, compared with countries of similar income levels.

As we enter the second decade of the twenty-first century, future global growth and competitiveness in China depend crucially on the development of knowledge and technology-based industries and services. Governments in many parts of the world have recognized that advancement in science and technology and innovation, instead of energy and resource abundance, in combination with an educated labor force, underpin sustained economic growth and prosperity through production upgrading and energy and resource efficiency. Although China has become the second largest economy in the world, it lags behind in its development of knowledge-intensity and high-technology industries and services, compared with OECD and major Asian economies. China must advance to the second-stage transformation—moving from resource- and energy-intensive, low value-added manufacturing to higher value-added industries, conserving energy and increasing reliance on renewable energy sources. In this respect, the experience of Korea provides some useful lessons for China to avoid repeating the middle-income trap that many Latin American countries experienced between 1975 and 2000.

One important aspect of the quality of growth, the environmental and resource sustainability, is often sidelined in the economic growth discourse. Global evidence, including China's growth experience, has shown that a global economy based on current patterns of consumption and production is simply not sustainable. China's three decades of growth have resulted in serious environmental and resource degradation. In 2007, China surpassed the United States to become the largest greenhouse gas emitter. Widespread water and air pollution and severe water scarcity will bring catastrophic consequences to the Chinese population and its future generations. While some environmental and resource degradation might be reversible, the potentially enormous cost of cleaning up must be borne by future generations who may be forever deprived of the opportunities to live in a safe and clean environment and in an ecosystem with biodiversity.

Environmental and resource degradation brought about by the past three decades' growth-focused development can also impede future economic growth. Serious water shortages in China are already a limiting factor in sustaining agricultural production, in supporting the capacity of water bodies to serve their ecological function, and in meeting the goal of reducing carbon emissions from clean coal use and the development of hydropower capacity.

The Chinese experience shows that an overwhelming focus on the pace of economic growth, with inadequate concern for the quality of growth, can hinder economic development or even reverse social progress. More alarmingly, the blind pursuit of rapid growth can eventually bring a country to the brink of an environmental catastrophe, limiting any prospect of future growth and harming the welfare of its population. Thus, in its 12th Five-Year Plan for 2010–2015, the Chinese government has set development targets to move China onto a growth path that is inclusive, equitable, sustainable, and green.

In sum, this case study's key message is that a focus on the quality of growth can achieve the goal of development and improve well-being. This message is *not* new. Over the past few decades, policymakers have been advised repeatedly that economic growth, poverty reduction, equity, and environmental and resource sustainability must be integrated into their national development strategies. In reality, however, as illustrated in China's three decades of growth, pursuing fast growth at all costs has always been the single most important national policy, overriding other development objectives and social concerns. Sensible answers explaining this contradiction likely come from an analysis of political economy, since policymaking is intrinsically a political process determined by as much political factors as economic ones, but that is beyond the scope of this book.

Looking forward, this case study provides us with grounds for optimism about China's development over the coming decades. As history shows, in countries undergoing major economic transformation, rising inequality and social disparity are often unavoidable. The role of government, thus, becomes critical in mitigating the adverse impact of inequality and in maintaining equity as a goal of development. In recent years, the Chinese government has indeed demonstrated its capacity and commitment in addressing inequalities and promoting inclusive growth through the implementation of a wide range of social policies and programs in both rural and urban areas.

The government's determination to protect the environment, to conserve national resources and the ecosystem, and to address climate change also inspires confidence. The major policy shift toward environmental protection and conservation in the 12th FYP and the introduction and enforcement of a series of environmental regulations, together with the broad public participation in addressing environmental issues, demonstrate that China will be able to embark swiftly on a development path that is sustainable and green.

It is the hope of both the Chinese people and the rest of world to see a rising China that is both strong and harmonious, setting an example of successful social and economic transformation for other countries. Each country differs in terms of its economic and political institutions, resource endowments, history, and culture, factors which all play important roles in determining growth paths and development outcomes. The Chinese experience, however, can provide some important lessons for many developing countries in their efforts to promote growth and reduce poverty.

Appendices

Appendix 1: Growth Incidence Curve

Different inequality measures have different sensitivity with respect to different segments of the income distribution. For example, . Therefore, it is more informative to examine the impact of aggregate economic growth over a wide range of the distribution. One of the most useful tools is the growth incidence curve (GIC) (Ravallion and Chen 2004). The GIC traces the growth rate in income or consumption between two points in time at each percentile of the distribution. It presents the growth rate of income of the *p*th quantile at two points of time t and $t+1$. The formula is specified as follows:

$$gt(p) = \left[yt(p) / yt - 1(p) \right] - 1$$

Letting p vary from zero to one, $gt(p)$ traces out the GIC. For example, at the 50th percentile, the figure gives the growth rate of the median income.

If there is no change in inequality, $gt(p) = \gamma t$ for all p, where γ equals the average growth rate in mean income, μ. Also, $gt(p) > \gamma t$ if and only if $yt(p)/\mu t$ is increasing over time. If $gt(p)$ is a decreasing (increasing) function for all p, then inequality falls (rises) over time for all inequality measures satisfying the Pigou-Dalton transfer principle.

If the GIC lies above zero everywhere, $g_t(p) \geq 0$ for all p, then there is first-order dominance of the distribution at date t over t-1. If the GIC is above the zero axis at all points up to some percentile p^*, then poverty has fallen for all headcount indices up to p^* (for all poverty lines up to the value that yields p^* as the headcount index) and for all poverty measures within a broad class (applying a result found in Atkinson 1987). If the GIC switches sign, then one cannot in general infer whether higher-order dominance holds by looking at the GIC alone (World Bank 2000).

Caution must be taken in interpreting the GIC as the results depend on the types of data source used in constructing GIC. For example, an upward sloping GIC does

X. Wang et al., *The Quality of Growth and Poverty Reduction in China*, International Research on Poverty Reduction, DOI 10.1007/978-3-642-36346-7,

not necessarily lead to the conclusions that individuals who were at the bottom end of the income distribution in the initial period benefited less than those at the higher end of the distribution. This is because an individual who was poor in the first period (e.g., in the 10th percentile) may move to the 55th percentile in the second period, but we could not observe this change in the absent of panel data that track individuals over time.

Appendix 2: A Review of Pro-poor Growth Literature

Over the past few years, pro-poor growth has become a very popular topic among policymakers and development practitioners. In many cases, it remains unclear what does it mean by pro-poor growth. Lopez (2004) provides a survey of the existing literature on this. Below is taken mainly from the review paper by Lopez (2004).

What do we mean by pro-poor growth? A number of international organizations have broadly defined pro-poor growth as growth that leads to significant reductions in poverty (OECD 2001). The first definition would basically require that the income share of the poor population increases for a growth pattern to be regarded as pro-poor. The simpler version of this definition is based on a relative concept of inequality and would simply state that the growth rate of the income of the poor is greater than the average growth rate (White and Anderson 2000). Thus (relative) inequality would fall with growth whenever growth is pro-poor. A more radical criterion (also proposed by White and Anderson 2000) would require that the share of the poor in the income increase is at least as large as their population share. This version is much more difficult to meet in practice and would require that (absolute) inequality declines.

The second definition of pro-poor growth is much less strict and focuses solely on the link between poverty and growth: growth is pro-poor if it reduces poverty (Ravallion and Chen 2004). Note that this definition would consider a growth episode as pro-poor if poverty falls regardless of the developments on the inequality front.

A third version of this definition is proposed by Kakwani and Pernia (2000) which is based on the comparison of the changes in poverty due to growth alone (i.e., holding inequality constant) and changes in poverty that take into account the actual changes in inequality. The authors refer to the ratio of these two elements as the pro-poor growth index, and an episode would be considered as pro-poor when the index is greater than 1 (i.e., when inequality falls).

Although intuitively appealing, this definition of pro-poor growth presents some limitations, particularly when applied in an operational context. First, pro-poor growth under this definition would be equated with inequality-reducing growth. However, by focusing so heavily on inequality, a policy package seeking an outcome that is consistent with this definition could lead to suboptimal outcomes for both poor and nonpoor households. For example, a society attempting to achieve pro-poor growth under this definition would favor an outcome characterized by average income growth of 2 % where the income of poor households grew by 3 %, over an outcome where average growth was 6 %, but the incomes of poor households grew by only 4 %. While the distributional pattern of growth favors poor households in the first scenario, both poor and nonpoor households are better off in the second scenario. Second, this definition might favor public sector interventions that reduce inequality regardless of their impact on growth.

Overall, there are two broad definitions of pro-poor growth, and the main distinction between them is whether for a given growth episode they focus on inequality outcomes (White and Anderson 2000; Kakwani and Pernia 2000) or instead on poverty outcomes (Ravallion and Chen 2004).

Policy debate and policy research on growth, income inequality, and poverty have three strands of focuses. First, they focus on the relative contribution of income growth and changes in inequality on poverty. The issue is relevant because knowledge about their relative importance is useful for designing policies that aim to achieve the right balance between pro-poor and pro-growth interventions.

The second strand concerns the growth-inequality relationship, in particular, the causal relationship between the two. These studies have attempted to identify the existence of the trade-offs between reducing inequality and improving growth performance, as opposed to a virtuous circle in which growth leads to lower inequality, and lower inequality in turn fosters faster growth.

The third strand concerns less with the poverty-growth-inequality triangle referred by Bourguignon (2004), instead more with the policies that countries should pursue in a successful poverty reduction strategy. This is motivated by the logics that poverty outcomes will depend on how a given policy affects growth and inequality. Therefore, assessing how appropriate a particular policy is for a poverty reduction strategy will require knowledge about the links between policies and growth as well as inequality.

Appendix 3: Highlights of the New Development Outline for the Automobile Industry

	Summary
Production expansion	
1	Targets have been set at 10 % annual growth in vehicle production and sales for the next 3 years and in the manufacturing and sale of ten million cars in 2009.
2	By 2011, passenger vehicles with engine capacity of below 1.5 l are expected to account for 40 % of market share, with those below 1.0 l taking 15 % of the market.
Mergers and acquisitions	
3	Two to three large auto giants with production and sales capacities reaching two million, and four to five smaller auto giants with capacities reaching one million are expected to be developed by 2011.

(continued)

(continued)

	Summary
Domestic consumption	
4	The purchase tax for vehicles with engine capacities below 1.6 l would be reduced to 5 % from 10 % between January 20 and December 31, 2009.
5	The government is expected to allocate 5 billion *yuan* in one-off allowances to farmers who replace their three-wheeled vehicles and low-speed trucks with minivans or buy new minivans with engine capacities below 1.3 l.
6	A discount of 10 % will be given to farmers who buy a minivan or light truck between March 1 and December 31, 2009, with a ceiling subsidy of 5,000 *yuan*.
7	Farmers who scrap their old three-wheeled vehicles or low-speed trucks will be able to enjoy 2,000 and 3,000 *yuan* subsidies, respectively, during the same period.
Technological upgrading	
8	The state aims to spend ten billion *yuan* on special investments to support auto enterprises in technological upgrading, such as developing new car engines using alternative energies and recycling battery sets.
9	It is envisaged that vehicles manufactured by domestically independent companies will account for more than 40 % of the total auto market; these vehicles will make up 10 % of overall export production and sales.
Development of alternative energy vehicle	
10	The production and sales of electronic vehicles are expected to achieve scale economy status by 2011. The combination of hybrid and pure electricity-driven vehicles is to achieve a production capacity of half a million by 2011, and the sales of passenger cars with new engines have been set at 5 % of total passenger vehicles sales.

Source: National Development and Reform Commission, *the People's Republic of China*, 2009

Appendix 4: *Ambitious State Plans on Green-Energy Vehicles*

The Chinese central government has realized that long-term competitiveness and sustainable development for the automobile industry lie in the promotion of green-energy technology. Wan Gang, Minister for Science and Technology, who was a former technical manager in the Production and Planning Department of the German Audi Corporation, has been influential in promoting green-energy technology and development of alternative fuel vehicles in China. On various occasions, he has reiterated in speeches that the central government will speed up the development of alternative energy vehicles to cope with the global financial crisis and enhance long-term industrial competitiveness.

As an important part of the central government's ambition to develop green-energy technology and expand the production of alternative energy vehicles 60,000 alternative fuel cars on the road and energy-saving and alternative energy vehicles 10 % of total annual auto output by 2012. Various means of financial support, from tax benefits to direct subsidies, are expected to be offered to carmakers engaging in the production of alternative fuel vehicles and to domestic consumers purchasing green-energy cars.

(continued)

(continued)

In new efforts to support the development of green-energy vehicles, the Ministry of Finance and Ministry of Science and Technology have jointly launched a trial program and given subsidies to thirteen Chinese municipalities to purchase hybrid and electric vehicles, for public transportation services (e.g., bus, taxi, and postal service cars). These 13 trial municipalities include Beijing, Shanghai, Chongqing, Changchun, Dalian, Hangzhou, Jinan, Wuhan, Shenzhen, Hefei, Changsha, Kunming, and Nanchang.
The local governments have also been adopting various strategies to promote the development of new energy vehicles by direct subsidies for green-energy vehicles purchases. For example, between 2010 and 2011, Shanghai's authority is expected to provide up to 20 % subsidies for purchases of new vehicles which have energy savings of 15 % and above. However, the Chinese leaders are overwhelmingly optimistic regarding the future development of alternative energy vehicles. Although the state has been encouraging domestic consumption of small-engine, low-emission vehicles and new energies, concrete results have yet to become apparent.
The promotion of new energy-fueled vehicles is costly, while average retail prices are still too expensive. Only when environmentally friendly vehicles and their associated alternative energies become affordable for the ordinary people will domestic consumption shift from gas-guzzling to energy-saving and environmentally friendly cars. Moreover, for the purely electricity-driven and hybrid vehicles, there is a lack of working proposals to address the issue of supporting infrastructure (e.g., electricity-recharging network). For many municipalities, building electricity-charging ports for recharging electric and hybrid vehicles will create financial difficulties; as a result, meeting operational needs will take many years.

Source: "60,000 alternative-energy vehicles to hit roads by 2012", *Xinhua News*, http://www.chinadaily.com.cn/china/2009-03/19/content_7597301.htm

"Greener cars get cash infusion", *China Daily*, online edition: http://www.chinadaily.com.cn/bizchina/2009-05/20/content_7794342.htm

"Hopes for Chinese rescue reined in", *Financial Times*, p. 18, April 21, 2009

References

Atkinson A (1987) On the measurement of poverty. Econometrica 55:749–764

Bloom D, Canning D, Hu L, Liu Y, Mahal A, Yip W (2006) Why has China's economy taken off faster than India's?. Presented at the 2006 Pan Asia conference. Available at http://scid.stanford.edu/events/PanAsia/Papers/papersonly.html

Brautigam D (2008) China's African aid: transatlantic challenges. German Marshall Fund of the United States, Washington, DC

Brautigam D (2010) China, Africa, and the international aid architecture, Working paper no. 107. African Development Bank, Tunis

China Human Development Report (2005) China Development Research Foundation, Beijing China

China National Bureau of Statistics (2010) China statistical yearbook. NBS, Beijing

China National Bureau of Statistics (2009) China statistical yearbook. NBS, Beijing

Collier P (2007) The bottom billion: why the poorest countries are failing and what can be done about it. Oxford University Press, New York

Dollar D, Shang J (2007) Das (Wasted) Kapital: firm ownership and investment efficiency in China, NBER working paper no. 13103. National Bureau of Economic Research, Cambridge, MA

Fu X, Balasubramanyam VN (2003) Township and village enterprises in China. J Dev Stud 39(4):27–46

Galor O, Tsiddon D (1997) Technological progress, mobility, and economic growth. Am Econ Rev 87:363–382

Goñi E, López JH, Serven L (2008) Fiscal redistribution and income inequality in Latin America, Policy research working paper, 4487. World Bank, Washington, DC

Hausmann R, Pritchett L, Rodrik D (2004) Growth accelerations. NBER working paper series. Working paper 10566. http://www.nber.org/papers/w10566

Hsueh T, Li Q (eds) (1999) China's national income, 1952–1995. Westview, Boulder

Judd (1985) Redistributive taxation in a simple perfect foresight model. J Public Econ 28(1985):59–83, North-Holland

Kakwani N, Pernia E (2000) What is pro-poor growth? Asian Dev Rev 18:1–16

Knight J, Ding S (2010) Why has China grown so fast? The role of physical and human capital formation. Oxf Bull Econ Stat 73(2):141–174

Lin JY (1988) The household responsibility system in China's agricultural reform: a theoretical and empirical study. Econ Dev Cult Change 36(3):S199–S224

Lin JY (2013) Against the consensus: reflections on the great recession. Cambridge University Press, Cambridge/New York

Lopez H (2004) Pro-poor-pro-growth: is there a trade off? The World Bank, policy research working paper no. 3378. World Bank, Washington, DC

X. Wang et al., *The Quality of Growth and Poverty Reduction in China*, International Research on Poverty Reduction, DOI 10.1007/978-3-642-36346-7,

López RE, Thomas V, Wang Y (2008) The quality of growth: fiscal policies for better results, IEG working paper 2008/6. World Bank, Washington, DC
Maddison A (1998) Chinese economic performance in the long run. Development Centre of the OECD, Paris
National Bureau of Statistics of China (Various years) China statistical yearbook (Zhongguo tongli nianjian). China Statistical Publishing House, Beijing
Naughton B (1995) Growing out of the plan: Chinese economic reforms 1978–1993. Cambridge University Press, Cambridge
New Directions for Crowded Cities (2010) J Trans Land Use 3(3):5–25
OECD (2001) The DAC guidelines poverty reduction. Organisation for Economic Co-operation and Development, Paris
OECD Economic survey of China (2007) OECD, Paris
Ravallion M, Chen S (2004) China's (Uneven) progress against poverty, World Bank policy research working paper no. WPS 3408. World Bank, Washington, DC
Shuzhuo Li (2006) Female child survival in China: past, present, and prospects for the future. Paper prepared for CEPED-CICRED-INED seminar on female deficit in Asia: trends and perspectives, Singapore, 5–7 December 2005
Sicular T, Yue X, Gustafsson B, Shi L (2007) The urban–rural income gap and inequality in China. Rev Income Wealth 53(1):95–128
Tang et al (2008) Tackling the challenges to health equity in China. Lancet 372(9648):1493–1501. doi:10.1016/S0140-6736(08)61364-1
Thomas V, Dailami M, Dhareshwar A, López RE, Kaufmann D, Kishor N, Yan Wang (2000) The quality of growth. Oxford University Press, New York
Thomas V, Yan Wang (2010) Fiscal policies for the quality of growth: implications. IPRCC working paper. November 2010, Beijing, China
UNDP (2008) Pro-poor macroeconomic policy: lessons from the Asia-pacific region, Millennium development goals initiative. UNDP Regional Centre in Colombo, Sri Lanka
Wan G (2004) Accounting for income inequality in rural China a regression-based approach. J Comp Econ 32(2004):348–363
Wan G (2007) Understanding regional poverty and inequality trends in China: methodological issues and empirical findings. Rev Income Wealth 53(1):25–59
Wan G, Lu M, Chen Z (2006) The inequality–growth nexus in the short and long run: empirical evidence from China. J Comp Econ 34(2006):654–667
Wei Li, Taye Mengistae, Lixin Colin Xu (2011) Diagnosing development bottlenecks: China and India. World Bank policy research working paper 5641. World Bank, Washington, DC
White H, Anderson A (2000) Growth vs. redistribution: does the pattern of growth matter? DFID white paper on eliminating world poverty: making globalisation work for the poor, London
Woo WT (1997) Chinese economic growth: sources and prospects. In: Fouquin M, Lemoine F (eds) The Chinese economy. Economica, London, p 1998
Woo WT (1998) Chinese economic growth: sources and prospects. In: Fouquin M, Lemoine F (eds) The Chinese economy. Economica, London
Young A (2003) Gold into base metal: productivity growth in the People's Republic of China during reform. J Pol Econ 111(6):1220–1261
Yu M, Wang X (2012) Inclusive growth of China's economy: measurement and evaluation. Econ Rev 3:30–38
Zeng, J, Bigsten A, Angang Hu (2006) Can China's growth be sustained? A productivity perspective. Unpublished paper. http://www.handels.gu.se/epc/archive/00005194/01/gunwpe0236.pdf

FSC
www.fsc.org
MIX
Papier aus verantwortungsvollen Quellen
Paper from responsible sources
FSC® C105338

If you have any concerns about our products, you can contact us on
ProductSafety@springernature.com

In case Publisher is established outside the EU, the EU authorized representative is:
Springer Nature Customer Service Center GmbH
Europaplatz 3, 69115 Heidelberg, Germany

Printed by Libri Plureos GmbH
in Hamburg, Germany